BLUE GLAZED PORCELAIN WARE OF YUAN

FORWARD

Yuan Dynasty is a Dark Age in Chinese history governed by Mongolian regime over the whole country of China. China was a strong country in history during the stage of Ching and Han. Her power was lasted until Five Northern Tributes agitation in Jing Dynasty which were just a short period of occupation of North China and afterwards, civilization assimilating ended their control entirely. Mongolian established the Empire covering whole area of China, but they are warriors and cavalries as well as arrow shooters. Their aggression did cause headache at the border of Southern Sung Dynasty, consequently, the strong Chinese warriors gradually turned weaken by continuous invasion of Liao, West Hsia and Chin. Mongolian took the advantage after defeated West Hsia and Chin and shiftied their target of conquering Southern Sung. Over the great victory of Southward expedition war, they policywisely governed with heavy press on Han people especially the pottery industry after their realizing its profitable business by utilizing Han labors' workmanship to trade the merchandise with Middle East.

Illustration of this subject is limited to Blue Glaze porcelain wares only, but Mongolian Yuan ruled China only about 90 years owing to their under maturity of civilization, the serious dispute in Palace and natural disaster caused terrible political upset and financial weary made the starved peasantry a rebellion followed by a subvert of the Mongolian government in China. The outstanding success of Blue Glaze reflects a splendid workmanship during the transmissional stage of Yuan / Ming, even up to Ching Dynasty, Blue Glaze Porcelain Wares are still recognized as a significant page of Chinese Porcelain History. Ming Blue is so familiar and welknown among Western Collectors. The era of Hung Wu is reputed with Blue and Underglazed Red, also the latter era of Yung Lo, Shien Teh, Cheng Hua, Chia Jing and Wan Li are all shinning with such product. Even in Kang Hsi of early Ching Dynasty when Western Enamel Color was introduced to China, Blue Glaze wares are still maintaining her important position in porcelain field of China.

中國歷代青花瓷精選集

Selections of Chinese Historical Blue Glaze Porcelain

To All Our Honorable Customers,
We are cordially inviting your pleasure who are public or private museum and are of high interesting with Chinese Ancient Cultural Items to contact us directly for our service via communication as follows :

SUNRISE INTERNATIONAL PUBLICATION CORP.
B1, 88 Chung Hsiao E. Rd. Sec.2, Taipei, Taiwan, R.O.C.
Telephone：886-2-396-5756
Fax : 886-2-351-6279
E-Mail：sunrises@ ms8.hinet.net
P.O.Box : 84-179 Taipei,Taiwan,R.O.C.

歡迎全球愛好中國古文物之公私立博物館〈美術館〉暨收藏人士如對本專輯內古文物有意珍藏，敬請來信或傳真給我們，我們將樂於服務。
來信暨傳真請惠寄下列地址：

東業國際圖書出版股份有限公司
台灣省 臺北市忠孝東路2段88號B1
TEL：886-2-396-5756 FAX：886-2-351-6279
電子信箱：sunrises@ms8..hinet.net
郵政信箱：台北市84-179 王興祖收

前言

　　元朝是我國歷史上受北方蒙古族佔領建立的一個全國一統的異族王朝。中國歷史自秦漢強盛國勢以後，到了晉朝時期才開始異族入侵的五胡亂華。但都是為時短暫和各族局部的侵佔，所以最後還是被華夏文化所席捲同化了。元朝是佔有全部中華版圖的時代，漠北的游牧民族，向以獷騎馳騁，嫻於戰射，自古為中國北方邊境的大患。至南宋時適逢南方漢人皇朝累年來受困於遼、金、西夏等的欺壓，國勢日漸衰微。蒙古人於是崛起，在消滅金及西夏以後，終以強兵壓境，結束了趙宋的漢人皇朝而建立大元帝國。他們用高壓政策，抑制漢人，尤其在瓷器生產方面，利用了漢人，瓷工的智慧和勞力，創出了對中東貿易的盈利，乃是本書所談元青花瓷中重要的因素。但是蒙元的全面統治中國祇有短短的九十餘年，主要原因是文化教養的不夠。先是宮廷變亂，接著是政治日益腐化，災荒頻仍，吏治窳敗，財政失衡，激起了農民揭竿起事，終於把一個大帝國輕易地推翻了。元代的青花瓷也為朱明初期輝煌的明初青花瓷開啟了燦爛的成績。一直到明、清甚至現代，青花瓷仍在中國瓷器史中，佔有重要的一頁。

　　明代青花瓷，在我國瓷器領域裡，佔了很重要的一章，如明初洪武的釉裡紅和青花，永樂、宣德、成化、嘉靖和萬曆各朝，都有青花瓷的輝煌一面。清代自康熙御窯以後致力於用西洋色料為主的琺瑯及粉彩等，但在三代官窯器上，仿前朝及自創特式的青花瓷，仍有它的地位。

　　為了展現元、明、清三代青花瓷光輝偉大的成就，我們經過一年多的努力，邀集多位收藏家，提供心愛珍藏，以饗海內外同好，也藉此讓前人的藝術結晶與世人共享。

青花瓷

青花瓷在中國曾經有過一段輝煌的時代，根據（一九七五）年在大陸揚州唐城遺址中發現的青花古瓷枕殘片，以及一九八三年又陸續發現的青花瓷碎片的出土，證明了在唐代末葉約當公元九世紀時已有青花瓷的問世。青花瓷是在素胎上先用一種氧化金屬煉製成的鈷藍顏料，以精細筆調，作畫在胎體上，然後澆上一層石英質的釉料，置入窯中以高溫約一三〇〇至一五〇〇度的熱度鍛燒，使釉的表面熔化成一種玻璃體。所謂的「胎為骨，釉為衣」就是整件瓷器最清楚的寫照。在釉層隔絕下的氧化金屬，會起物理還原作用而將顏料中的氧脫出，呈現出金屬元素的本質顏色。此項技術由於瓷工們經驗的累積，使在中國瓷器工業上造成了燦爛的青花瓷。這種所謂鈷藍的原料，原不是中國本地的土產，而是來自中東地區的礦物顏料。歷史上中國和中東地區的交通和貿易，在公元紀元前即已開始，到公元九至十世紀時適當唐代末葉，絲路交通的日漸頻繁。這種輸入的礦質鈷藍（COBALT BLUE）亦稱「回青」或「蘇泥渤青」的顏料，由於含化學物的鈷和若干錳、鐵、砷等成份，使所繪出的青花顯出不同的深淺，濃處如靛，淺處如天藍色，並有鐵銹斑點。在最早唐代青花殘片上已給人鮮艷奪目的感覺。

談到回青、蘇泥渤青顏料，產自遙遠的中東，為什麼要長途跋涉帶到中國來燒造在瓷器上呢？事實上在伊拉克薩馬拉（SAMARRA）即出土公元九世紀前的當地藍綠釉器，器上即繪有鈷藍顏料燒出的紋飾，但胎質粗鬆，係一種當地的化妝土，紋飾亦非釉下彩而是釉中加鈷藍彩燒成，紋飾更是充滿阿剌伯風味，此種藍釉介於陶、瓷之間的器物，在九至十世紀後即少製造，可能受中國西運瓷器的影響。中東地區出產這種極合適燒瓷顏料的鈷藍，但沒有像中國土地上所產的瓷石原料，也沒有訓練出燒造瓷器的技術環境如工匠、燃料等。所以使他們本地所產的陶瓷工業沒落，而在一千多年前因為對青花瓷的喜愛，不惜將

藍顏料由商旅駝隊帶到中國，在鞏縣地方的窯場燒造出青白色的瓷器，再經絲路由駱駝捆載運到波斯、伊拉克轉運至中東各地。以往唐宋瓷器中的單色釉都是由含鐵的青色，含銅的紅色，但由氧化鈷所發的藍色，其強度穩定。唐代最早期的青花瓷由鞏縣窯用中東鈷藍燒出的已達到很好的成績。可惜在唐朝覆亡後，中國的中原地區，適當五代紛亂時代，絲路的貿易切斷，鈷藍的來源也絕跡，而使鞏縣造瓷的窯業也停頓了，一直到北宋初年，由於在浙江龍泉金沙塔塔基出土了一隻青花碗是太平興國二年埋入的，但是胎質粗鬆且帶灰色，釉色不夠透明而帶青白，青花色澤深具灰黯的感覺。北宋立國一六七年，造瓷工業冠絕各代，但始終未見青花瓷之出現，事實上絲路已斷，鈷藍之輸入受阻，也是主要原因。金沙塔出土的青花碗，色澤灰澀，恐即嘗試採用浙江礦石藍而未成功的事實。這樣到了南宋末年的咸淳年間，也見到製作成功的青花瓷，一件出土於紹興的環翠塔青花瓷及在於民國八十四年五月間在台北東業拍賣中的咸淳年號青花三管瓶，恐也是採取浙江本地產平等青顏料較成功的嘗試。但其發色總不及進口鈷藍的明艷。

元代蒙古鐵騎遠征及中東，橫跨歐亞，一時武力稱雄，軍中有攜帶鈷藍原料返回中原者，於是為老瓷工嚮往的鈷藍（蘇泥渤或回青）又重現眼前，乃在景德鎮繪瓷，用釉下彩燒造成功，從此元青花瓷又一度綻放異彩於中國造瓷工藝了。元人是獷騎出身的游牧民族，入據中原，併吞南宋後，用高壓欺凌漢族的政策來統治中華。但對造瓷窯工尚為優待，由此可知蒙古統治者的重視瓷器工業，不外乎由於爭取外貿利益，而瓷器出口是一項大宗收入。試看一直到今天近東及歐洲的公私博物院中仍收藏著大量的元代青花瓷，如伊朗的阿耳代比耳廟（ARDEBIL SH）及土耳其伊斯坦堡的脫普卡卜博物館所陳列的青花瓷，莫不質地堅緻潔淨，顏色靛青明亮，繪圖繁富，器型也多高大，數量更是眾多，足使中國人對瓷器之英文文字用CHINA稱為之驕傲。

蒙元宮庭用瓷也由景德鎮窯場供應，當時曾設立「浮梁瓷局」，而「樞府」窯件也即是貢給京師宮庭所用的瓷器，景德鎮造瓷負有二大使命，即貢瓷給宮庭方面所用，另即大量外銷給中東，以使維持元代政府財政上一大收益。元青花瓷和宋瓷是截然不同的另一種工藝，宋代的單色釉如汝、官、定、哥等都是單色晶瑩，造型古雅，大小適中，偶爾亦見窯燒中的變色所形成的多色花瓷如鈞窯的色彩，絕非描繪所成。但民間用器如磁州、長沙等窯，雖配以手繪紋飾但運筆樸拙，屬於民俗風味的作品，此外如定窯及耀州窯的刻劃花紋，那與青花瓷的繁密紋飾，更是另一種表現了。但是元青花器的體積又帶給人們一種大塊文章的感覺，如近今出土及中東許多博物館中竟全屬大件的元青花瓷，俗傳伊斯蘭回民習慣圍坐就餐，用手抓飯，故使用人件瓷盤，大碗盛湯較適宜。蒙古人亦為游牧民俗與阿剌伯習俗相近，故獵騎演武之餘，亦以大盤吃肉，大碗喝湯的使用器具是尚。青花瓷的元代作品以盤、罐、梅瓶、葫蘆瓶、玉壺春、扁瓶、執壺、鉢、碗、洗、高足杯及盞托等，以大件器為多。而且普遍的是胎體厚重，器底無釉但或有旋紋。器足內壁自上向下斜撇而外壁斜削成形，圈足施釉不到底，可見到露胎的褐紅色，圈足或呈彎扭狀，在大件器尤為突出。圈足內露胎處或粘有釉斑釉塊，罐、瓶之類均分段製胎，其接胎處有明顯接痕，而內壁多見淡紅、黃色釉層或赤褐斑或小黑點，高足杯杯身及杯足分別在濕胎時接合，足部空心不封底。元青花紋飾圖均屬瓷工以畫家筆法畫出精細的纏枝花卉如牡丹、蓮、菊或水藻、魚、龍、水禽等圖案，而且瓷坏直立時運筆，故多出現中峰筆法。圖有主體亦有輔助，主圖多在中腹、碗心、盤心，輔圖多在口、足沿等處。元青花瓷更有符合元曲版畫之人物故事畫，如蒙恬將軍，桃園結義，蕭何追韓信等。至於元青花採用滿佈主圖而輔以花草圖案的作法，不能不認為是受中東回教工藝紋飾的影響，往往密佈全器，不若明代青花之疏朗畫筆。談到中國瓷器，免不了要涉及「龍」的紋飾，元青花龍爪，大都僅三爪或四爪，因五爪之龍紋在元代至元二年曾禁令不可採為圖紋。

關於元青花器有二則故事，特提出來談談。

一、英倫大衛德基金博物館中的一對元青花象鼻雙耳雲龍大瓶一對，口頸有「信州路玉山縣順城鄉德教里荊塘社奉聖弟子張文進喜捨香爐花瓶一副祈保合家清吉子女平安至正十一年四月良辰謹見星源祖殿胡淨一元帥打供」六十二字之款識。這宗寶物是在一九三○年代，有江西人吳來熙攜這二件青花瓷到上海，先是為上海古玩商否定，稱是膺鼎，吳即北上故都，向琉璃廠探售，不料國人不識寶亦加以否定。他盤纏用馨流落北京郊區，寄宿一冷廟中僅此一對大瓶相伴。適逢英國大衛德爵士在故都搜求古物，竟被這位專家識出確屬元青花寶瓶，於是以相當代價，購入運至英國，直到今天仍站立在英倫大衛德基金博物館中。

二、青花瓷人物畫蕭何月下追韓信梅瓶是 九五九年在大陸南京附近江寧縣善橋鄉觀音山發掘明初黔寧昭靖王沐晟墓中出土的這件青花梅瓶。梅瓶的型式是口小肩腹部渾圓，向下腹削瘦。通體青花紋飾，輔以纏枝牡丹，雜以梅花、竹子、松樹、蕉葉、山石等於主圖蕭何月下追韓信故事圖之上部，下邊足沿處繪蓮紋，畫法層次分明，渾然一體。青色發色青翠濃豔，胎質潔白緊密，大陸考古人士斷為元代末年景德鎮燒造的精緻瓷器。現已入藏於南京市博物館。中共郵電部於一九九一年十月十一日發行的一套六枚景德鎮瓷專題郵票，即列入二十分面值此一梅瓶圖案。

元代瓷器，一般釉厚而垂，濃處或起條紋，淺處可見波紋，所稱之元龍泉及元鈞，均可依此參考之。元代統治者蒙古人，起於漠北，入據中原之地，其習性好勇尚武，時以勝利者心態及映在瓷型制上，如奇獸怪鳥及器附大耳等。元龍泉胎骨厚重，每在器上轉折處，作稜角及凹槽，圈足垂直，足底齊平，釉層較薄，色呈青黃。至於元代仿鈞，所燒出紅、紫二色，頗足稱道，尤其紫色後人名之為「元紫」。

元代瓷最享盛名者，當屬青花。雖然明代青花之水準超越元代多多，但講到青花瓷的成熟及揚名域外，當以後

4

大宗出口的項目，才堪推崇。元代宮廷亦大量使用青花瓷，且由官方設局 (浮梁瓷局) 掌控景德鎮附近所產瓷土及利用南宋以來熟練之瓷工，宮廷或官府所用燒瓷例用「樞府」二字為款。紋飾更採用劃、刻、印、貼、鏤堆等新穎手法。題材也採用創新的雷紋、鋸齒紋、方格紋等。型式更增添碗、盞、盤、皿、碟、壺、缽、洗、瓶、爐等，而且盤、洗、瓶等都有大件之燒造。格古要論載：「古人用湯瓶酒注，不用壺瓶及有嘴盂，至茶鐘壺盤，皆胡人所用。」中國人使用者始於元朝，故定、官窯俱無此器。可知古壺無嘴，元代始有之，而將無嘴者稱瓶。

元、明二代青花瓷因大量出口，聲名遠播，到了明代初期漸漸為西域胡人所喜愛。明實錄有一則稱：英宗正統時，光祿寺招宴西域人及女真人，宴後清點瓷器，被偷達五百八十多件。可見青花瓷之受夷人青睞，不惜在朝廷盛宴後挾帶瓷器而遁。

當時韃靼、女真及天方諸國 (中東地區) 人，都以販運瓷器為利藪，一次多至數十車，捆紮高達三丈。明沈德符「野獲篇」筆記中載有捆載磁器自景德鎮運出，先用桶裝艾草的方法，運到北京。然後在北京另行纏捆，排列整齊，將泥土和豆、麥種敷上捆紮。不時灑水，使豆、麥發芽生長，芽莖更鑽入隙縫生長，相互纏繞膠著，以致緊密牢固，擲地不碎，才能重車裝載西行，經絲路抵達中東。瓷器也有與茶葉共同包裝，防止散裂，又可兼顧瓷茶之出口，為中東市場所需的貨物。

明青花瓷外銷地有日本、朝鮮、南洋、中東、歐洲等地，影響義大利人在威尼斯之仿造，其法更傳遍荷蘭、英、法、德、俄等國。甚至也遣人來華學習燒造。甚至日本、朝鮮、越南、暹羅等地，亦都有青花瓷的燒製。

元明之間青花瓷

元青花瓷並非官窯器，此話怎麼解釋呢！因從未見有五爪龍，器面所描繪的龍，差不多都是三爪或四爪。本文前段曾提到：至元二年夏四月，元史順帝紀中所頒禁令中有禁服雙角五爪龍，甚至萬壽，福壽、赭黃色等服。足見元代造瓷，僅「樞府」窯器有五爪龍可推測屬官窯外，其他一概為民間用器或外銷瓷品。

元末明初的國祚轉變時期，青花瓷的燒造工業，轉變不大，景德鎮的瓷工，仍安其業。明太祖於初定天下，即成立御窯廠，使造瓷工業繼續生產。故洪武年代的青花瓷仍步元青花後塵的風格，惟青花色感較灰暗，或許當時中東鈷藍存量漸少。改採用含錳量高而含鐵量較低的國產顏料的混合。底部圈足改為整齊的平削替代了元代的斜削。

凡徑在二十公分左右的，已出現滿釉底，另梅瓶的口部亦由上窄下寬的梯形唇，改為筒形撇捲口，圖紋也較元青花為簡單，龍紋亦改採元代不用之五爪龍。青花梅瓶有洪武時期所燒造的在瓶肩部有「春壽」二篆字者，即因圖紋係五爪龍及口型撇捲而被斷為明代初期官窯器。綜合以上各點似乎明初所造的青花器，其工藝水準略遜於元青花，所以明初洪武一朝是青花瓷的衰退期。

近年在印尼、菲列濱等地，有若干青花瓷的小件器出土，高度均在五至七公分左右，間或有少數的釉裡紅，圖紋多為簡筆花草，且以菊花為主，由此可推測元、明時代青花器外銷地區，不限於中東，亦兼延伸及東南亞。但此種簡筆花草圖案青花，應屬於洪武時期之外銷瓷器。故可推測當鄭和船隊之浩浩蕩蕩經南洋西行以前，即有南洋之貿易海舶在通航，而鄭和則為較大規模的官方船隊而已。

明代的永樂、宣德二朝是青花瓷器的黃金時代，最主要原因是政治漸趨安定、富足的經濟也上軌道。窯工生活無缺，乃用盡工藝技巧，務求瓷品的細膩潔白，青花的艷麗。而且又有一種由鄭和從

南洋帶回的「蘇麻離」藍，含高鐵低錳的青料，最適宜燒造青花瓷，發色濃艷，略含鐵銹斑色。永樂青花一般均無款識，僅一種壓手杯上有「永樂年製」四字篆書。宣德時期才在青花瓷器上見有「宣德年製」及「大明宣德年製」二種款識，據說均出當時名書法家沈度手蹟。永樂青花瓷色濃而翠色欲滴，並有鐵銹斑泛現釉面。同樣的器物是永樂較輕而宣德較重。永樂釉肥白中泛青，少數有開片，且底足釉色特別潔白。青花釉色往往有暈散現象者，亦是永樂多過於宣德。在造型方面，永樂器以梅瓶、大盤、玉壺春、雙繫扁瓶、深身洗、缽、碟、罐、高足杯、碗及壓手杯較多見。永樂時代也有特創的型式，如天球瓶、單面扁壺、雙繫扁瓶、扁葫蘆型瓶、花澆、尖底蓮子碗、雙繫或多繫把壺及若干伊斯蘭型式執壺、筒型器等。且永樂時期造瓷有一特出的改革，即除開大盤、大壺外，在器底施釉，講明白些，辨別青花瓷器之器底施釉者是元、明永樂之分野的一項重要依據。永樂瓷杯之滑底沙足及宣德之釜底線足，與嘉靖之饅心圓足也是參考上的要點。永樂大件器雖器底不施釉，但胎質滑細，有糯米粉之滑潤感，在細砂底面，偶亦見小塊鐵斑及釉面呈波浪紋。另一較為明顯的永樂青花的圖案，改變了元代繁密多層次的佈局而趨向於空白色露出較多。圖案主題以梅花、牡丹、蓮花、菊花較多，輔以蕉葉、如意雲、回紋、波濤等，以疏朗筆法繪出，而且按雙鈎小筆填彩，顯現出濃淡不一的筆觸，不若前代之大筆一筆塗抹。

永樂與宣德青花瓷是我國青花生產的高峰，尤其宣德青花更是聲名籍甚，宣德器亦多於永樂器，但這二朝的時間相鄰近，祇有在下列幾點中去辨別永、宣二代青花瓷：

（一）宣德大部有「大明宣德年製」或「宣德年製」的官窯款。

（二）永樂青花色彩濃翠帶鐵斑者係進

口的蘇麻離青，色料中礦質成份錳低鐵高。同時期有用國產浙青料則錳高鐵低，故色澤帶灰而無鐵斑。但宣德器中有一種色澤偏淡而不呈灰暗，兼無鐵斑而具有一種逸雅靜穆的風味，可能是用進口和國產青料的混合而產生的效果。

（三）永樂宣德青花著彩均使用較小畫筆，勾勒時需多次重新蘸料，因此其色彩出現深淺相間的觸痕，故永宣器未見一筆塗末的畫法，凡一筆塗抹之畫法，即非永宣青花器。

（四）永宣青花瓷，白中泛青，凡瓶罐之屬，往往口足邊緣呈水綠色。

（五）永宣青花大件底亦不施釉，胎體白色含火石紅而於燒成後呈淺紅色瓷胎。但小件者圈足內施釉，且露胎者均無旋痕。清代仿宣德器往往見旋痕。

（六）宣德青花瓷大盤之底足外牆內斂，裡牆外斜，且以矮圈足為多，足之脊口每有楞角感，但後世仿品則滾圓呈泥鰍背狀。

（七）宣德瓶壺之類，胎體均係上下接合，其接痕由手觸立可感覺。清代及以後仿品則前後模製後拼合，其接縫也在器身二側，觸摸即可發現。

（八）宣德青花，型態最為繁多，如梅瓶、玉壺春瓶、貫耳瓶、折方瓶、葫蘆扁瓶、抱月瓶、僧帽壺、大罐、大缸、缽、燭台、豆、高足杯、花澆、渣斗、匜、蟋蟀罐、洗、碟、筆管、筆盒、水盂等。盤之大徑者很多輸出土耳其及伊朗等地，所見有板沿、微侈口、菱口等三種。徑均在四十公分左右。回民喜團坐以手取食此種大盤，或即為回人習俗之適用而製以輸出者。

（九）圖紋之配合器型，似乎亦為宣德器中之特色，前述板沿大盤則配以把蓮、纏枝葡萄、瓜果及纏枝菊為多。在微侈口大盤上則多見把蓮、串枝蓮及牡丹。而在菱口盤上則例繪纏枝蓮為主。宣德龍亦改變元代龍之細長頸而代之以豎髮、披髮，且神態兇猛，爪尖呈帶圓圈。另並有雙鳳、獅球、波濤海獸等圖，出現於紋飾。宣德青花之輔圖紋飾，常見覆蓮瓣紋，瓣心填色而絕無元代風格。蕉葉紋主胍二線間不填色亦屬宣德窯特式，回文也是以整圈連環型式，而纏枝花、勾雲紋、如意雲、波濤紋、斜方

格、錦地紋、團龍、團鳳、及開光立龍和蓮托八寶紋也都採用上宣德青花瓷器。

宣德瓷中更有一種藍地白花，係由器物內、外壁錐劃出圖案花紋，再高溫一次燒成。此種藍地釉下彩，與鈷料呈色劑之藍釉不同。另有一種印花裝飾，盛行於洪武時代，至永樂已少見，宣德瓷中有內印龍紋，外繪蓮池游龍青花小盤，為景德鎮御窯廠遺址中出土僅見之品。

明沈德符著「敝帚齋餘譚」一書中稱：「本朝窯器，用白地青花間裝五色，為古今之冠。如宣窯品最貴，近日又重成窯，出宣窯之上。」沈德符為萬曆間人，與宣、成相隔百年，對青花加彩瓷已如此推崇，五百年後今天，當更珍貴。此種青花及釉下二重加彩精美瓷器，當時製作既少，至今傳世更稀，一般清代仿青花加彩之官窯，甚為人重視。

明代瓷業，在正統、景泰、天順（一四三六～一四六四）的二十八年間是官窯瓷的衰退期，當其時製作粗陋，圖案仍以纏枝、折枝為主，間亦有亭台樓閣，每繪如置於雲霧幻景中，人物鼻尖凸出，柳條如斷續雨點。故此時期都是民間窯的市場。天順款僅山西博物館藏有「天順七年大同馬氏造」一件青花爐及香港有「天順年」回文香爐，款式書法均較拙劣。

成化又是明代瓷器的復興期，尤其是彩色燒瓷的振興，成化時期的青花官窯器，亦屬青花瓷中為後世珍視的原因，況且傳世絕少，燒造精美。其原因有下列各點：

（一）所用青料為國產被塘青（亦稱平等青），產於江西樂平，發色淡雅，而無鐵斑。

（二）器型一變前期永、宣時期的大型器物而傾向於輕巧小件，雖顏色有偏青及偏白二種，但足底釉色與器身釉色一律，僅器物底部釉面，稍呈波浪式。

（三）器物底部或圈足有所謂米糊底，撫之較為粗糙者屬成化早期窯燒，較平滑如米糊者，當屬成化後期產品。

(四) 成化器畫風,以雙鉤線條,顯然地改變了宣德時期的一筆畫出畫風。

(五) 圖紋以龍鳳、團龍、團鳳、波濤獸、蓮花八寶、嬰戲、三友、花蝶、花鳥及梵文點綴外,有一種十字杵圖為明初前代所未有之圖案。龍嘴唇上翹,偶銜一蓮花,龍身有飛翼,有前爪而無後爪以及花草加上樹石欄干,皆為成化器中青花瓷之特出圖紋。

(六) 成化器釉面小氣泡密集而整齊,不若宣德釉面下大小氣泡之不規則排列。

(七) 成化款字以「大明成化年製」六個楷字直書隻行為多,青花器亦置款於雙圈藍色者為多,間有方欄及單圈款,則較少見。成化偽款較多,前人有詩句詮釋:大字尖圓頭非高,成字撇硬直倒腰,化字人匕平微頭,製字衣橫少越刀。為鑑賞人士所重視的參考依據。

成化青花民瓷質較粗糙,色澤青中偏灰,與官窯相差甚遠。所採用圖案仍不脫前朝風尚,有攜琴訪友之人物畫及樹石庭院之風景畫。

弘治青花仍是成化時代的沿續,但存世瓷器少於成化瓷,因那時代的青花原料,起了一些改變,即採用國產平等青,其色澤成為青色偏淡,畫風也偏重一筆塗抹,圖紋以龍為多,如蓮池游龍、雲龍、九龍、飛翼龍、雙龍搶珠及花果或配以梵文等紋飾。

至於弘治民窯青花瓷仍屬粗糙,但圖案取題較廣,如梅、竹、松鶴、水藻蓮花等。釉色白中泛灰青,釉面下氣泡小而整齊密集。官窯款識為「大明弘治年製」二直行六楷字,外圍藍釉雙圈,治字三點,低於台字。清康熙仿品則治字三點與台字均齊平矣。弘治器有一特點,凡盤類都呈塌底凹形。

正德青花官窯,胎體較厚重,以文房用具為多,釉面亮而色青。大碗口沿厚釉處更青,青色呈藍灰乃石子青的特色。正德青花既不若宣德時之濃翠,亦乏成化器之淡雅。其畫法又恢復成化時之雙勾填色,且用長筆平塗成較

弱的筆觸感。但到了正德後期,開始用一種進口之回青色料,發色濃翠,略泛紫紅,釉面內小氣泡密集呈魚子狀。圖案則見到了頗具特出的纏枝、折枝花卉及魚、馬等。款字亦為雙行「大明正德年製」字或「正德年製」四字款,且有橫直不同之排列。

明代嘉、隆、萬三朝青花瓷

嘉靖在位四十五年,據說在這漫長的歲月裡,官窯產量多達六十萬件,前朝亦遺留未燒完成器物三十餘萬件,此一近百萬件瓷器中,當然也佔相當數量的青花瓷。嘉靖時,因江西贛半地區不寧,陂塘青燒瓷色料不易取得,於是轉向西域貢品中專要回青,使此一時期的青花,發色濃翠豔麗。同時尚有一種國產石子青料,由窯工研究出這二種青料混合使用,不單顏色清亮,更透出豔麗之感。傳說正德年間大璫曾自雲南取得燒瓷回青料,因青料名貴,工匠每多藏匿私取,浮梁縣令乃規定劑量之法,命以九回一石造官窯御器,民用常器則僅四回六石。故嘉窯之青翠可愛,頗受稱揚。其時饒州鮮紅土亦已絕跡,因之嘉靖器之露胎處,已少見紅土,亦無里鐵斑之出現,惟青花之青色略泛紫紅,而且釉光亮,一般底足均甚規整。至於嘉靖民窯則不用或少滲合回青料,故製作粗厚草率,瓷胎接痕明顯,釉色缺乏滋潤感。

嘉靖青花器在型式上也有較大的改變,如玉壺春腹部肥大、執壺扁而頸細長,更有一代特出的造型如葫蘆瓶、方斗、方蓋盂形罐及出戟尊、爵等器,皆所謂蘸壇祭器。至於紋飾方面,除龍鳳花卉外,又見嬰戲、魚藻、禽鳥、人物、山水、草字福壽等。嘉靖民窯器見有八卦、雲鶴、八仙等圖案,當屬嘉靖崇尚道教有關。而正面龍紋圖案又顯出時代性的特式。

嘉靖款書亦為二行六字,有青花雙圈及無雙圈罐等。間或有環形款,橫或豎式款,但四字款之「嘉靖年製」者

較少見。康熙仿嘉靖青花六字中「大」、「年」、「製」三字均和康熙款極相似。隆慶短短六年，故官窯青花器絕少，特出之型式有提梁壺、銀錠盒及四方盒等，圖案以龍鳳團花為多，有六字款「大明隆慶年製」及「大明隆慶年造」二種。

萬曆朝長達四十八年，其青花官窯器可分前後二期，前期仍用回青，後期則改用浙青，因回青用罄，據天工開物載：「凡饒鎮所用以衢信二郡山中者為上料，名曰浙料，上高諸邑者為中，豐城諸處為下也」。可見萬曆後期所燒青花瓷，可能均用浙江青料。萬曆前期青花，出自回青，故發色濃豔，後期浙料則呈明快之狀，足見瓷匠之處理發色頗有其獨到之處。自明代萬曆後期至清康熙時，青花瓷曾有一度轉變性發展。此中經天啟、崇禎，雖僅少數典雅亮麗的官窯青花，但民窯的青花生產量極多，其中亦包括相當數量的出口瓷，輸往中東伊斯蘭地區，其青色均臻上乘。當時青花瓷器有四種用途：

一. 宮庭用官窯器。

二. 廟宇供器。

三. 專供外銷中東、歐洲及日本等地，有「五良大輔吳祥瑞造」款等特製品。

四. 一般民用器。

明末至清朝青花瓷

天啟、崇禎二朝之廟宇供器，傳世所見尚有年號款字。但沿及清初順治、康熙二朝青花器，在圖案上則創出一種奔放且符合當時文人畫及版刻藝術的風格，如有些在筆筒上的山水畫及近隸體的題字，亦有幾乎彷彿石濤之畫。此一明、清造瓷之轉承時期，英文稱（TRANSMISSION PERIOD），意即明代瓷工之繼續為新朝窯場效力，易代之際總有一種新氣象之感，故瓷上畫風稍轉奔放，亦意料中事。

康熙青花瓷的造型，以典雅稱勝，且以文房用具為多。圖案主題也不出龍鳳、纏枝蓮、雲鶴、吉祥、山水、花卉及仿古銅器紋、團龍、團鳳、團鶴等。康熙青花更多仿明代宣德、成化、嘉靖、萬曆之器，且仿其年號款識，不論官窯、民窯，其製作程度都具水準。均用浙江青料，用鍛燒法煉製，特顯現出鮮豔濃翠之感。同時在康熙瓷中出現了印花法也令人有凸出之感。圖案的特色在康熙漫長的時代中，也有若干自由奔放風味，如古文學的戲曲故事之秋聲賦、朱苔拜石、西廂、三國、風塵三俠等，咸由圖案畫出，當時民間也普遍風行青花瓷，故產量較多。

青花瓷土原料以高嶺土最足稱，產於江西浮梁新正都的麻倉山，明、清時淘洗最精，故釉底晶瑩如玉、堅而白淨，閃爍若金星。早期青花色料含微量鐵元素，故各時代帶不同程度青色，但此種微青色，到清代後期漸褪，到清末幾成無色透明體。

雍正青花較康熙為進步，以細緻精雅是尚。因利用浙青以改善加工，故青色中已無康熙青花之泛紫現象，由於施工技術進步及嚴謹，青花發色純正。在型式方面亦有些特出，如牛頭尊、貫耳大瓶、如意耳瓶、貫耳六方瓶、燈籠瓶等。款識為二直行楷書六字款及三行篆書方框仿宋體

四字款者較為普遍。

乾隆做了六十年的太平天子，青花官瓷的色澤和前朝雍正相同。型式以仿古銅器型及仿明代永樂、宣德、成化三朝器物為多。乾隆時督窯官唐英撰「陶冶圖說」謂浙青料出於浙江、金華二府，至於江西、廣東諸山產者，色薄不耐火，止可畫粗。乾隆青花之仿中東伊斯蘭器形也很普遍。其時，外銷瓷器之盛況，亦不減於元、明。而且青花瓷圖飾，崇尚繁縟，恐亦為迎合中東買家之口味。乾隆款識，較多見者為三直行六字篆書及方框仿宋體四字，其他則少見。

清代景德鎮造瓷工業，至嘉慶、道光時，已漸式微，偶見精細之作，但總不能超越雍、乾。到咸豐、同治二朝，適逢太平天國兵燹，景德鎮地屬戰區，造瓷幾陷停頓，青花瓷之燒造更是絕少。光緒一朝又稍恢復，頗不乏精細之製品，但格於迎合外銷之仿古潮流，於青花瓷之這項藝術，祇能說是到了夕陽餘暉的光景了。

釉裡紅

釉裡紅也是釉下彩繪於坯胎，早在唐代長沙窯瓷用的釉下銅料，其發色即為紅色也就是最早的釉裡紅。唐後經五代紛擾，二宋亦未見用銅料釉下彩燒造。一直要到元代景德鎮的窯工才悟出釉下用銅色料可燒出和青花瓷一樣的紅色的紋飾。甚至可以將鈷藍和銅色料分二次繪圖，然後施上一層透明釉，在高溫還原燄中一次燒出，即成為青中有紅色相間的圖案。在中國紅色一向為民俗上公認的吉利顏色，所以在青花器上出現了凝重華麗的雙彩色，當然更為受歡迎。

但是釉裡紅的發色比較困難，因氧化銅色料在燒造中易成飛紅（即紅色使圖案模糊），所以先用線繪，在線條範為內加彩，可是燒後仍呈飛紅。改用拔白即是圖案先在白胎面刻劃線條，在範圍內填彩燒造。仍不理想，於是採用所謂的圖繪，以銅紅料塊或片塗繪上圖案，使在鍛燒中不致抹糊圖案。似乎較勝於前二敷彩方法，傳世釉裡紅也以塗繪方法較為普遍，而以線繪最少。釉裡紅的燒造成功率不高每因飛紅或紅色太濃或淺而遭淘汰，故存世不多。惟此種瓷器在元代尚在技術上未臻成熟，色澤往往顯現淡而偏灰，部份且有飛紅甚至略呈暗黑顏色，釉面亦見開片。大部屬露胎糙底，除若干玉壺春瓶有釉底者。底足平削，圖紋以纏枝、牡丹、蓮、菊等為主。釉裡紅色料絕不如青花之易於控制，甚至可控深淺濃淡，繪出生動的人物故事。所以明初洪武以後釉裡紅器絕少人物圖。宣德高足杯有釉裡紅單魚圖紋，據稱色料中有紅寶石為末，紋飾凸起，寶光微現，乃當時御窯廠精心傑作。但此後到明代成化年間以後，或由於多彩瓷的出現，使釉裡紅瓷停止燒造，一直到清代康熙時才又見恢復。

江西饒州府浮梁縣西興鄉景德鎮附近所產瓷土燒造器物，胎薄釉潤，色白花青，元青花不失為一代製作。元時浮瓷局督造瓷器有「樞府」二字者，因質佳飾美，一般目為宮庭或貴族、顯宦所用之器。元青花因景德鎮大量燒造，不單宮庭，民間亦普遍使用。中東回教地區則有鉅大數量的輸往。近年有為數頗多之元青花出土紀錄，茲列舉若干，以為讀者對大陸出土資料，作些參考。

* 一九六○年南京出土明初沐晟墓中青花人物梅瓶，繪有蕭何追韓信圖，推測為洪武製品，恐仍為元代瓷匠作品。

* 一九六五年河北保定，發現一窖藏元青花大罐，八稜瓶、玉壺春及執壺等，共計六件。

* 一九七一年北京鼓樓大街，於元大都遺址出土青花碗、盤、杯、托子、瓢、壺等計十餘件。

* 一九七八年杭州挖出元代至元丙子年墓葬中，三座觀音坐像。

* 一九八○年九江墓葬中發現元代延祐已未青花塔蓋瓷瓶一件。

* 一九八一年江西豐城縣出土至元戊寅六月青花釉裡紅四靈蓋罐及瓷穀倉各一件。

關於青花瓷器在元代前期，尚未臻盛行，一直到十四世紀三十年代後，才出現了高潮。據元末孔齊所著「至正日記」載云：元末士大夫好宋瓷之定、官、哥窯及當時之御土窯（即樞府窯），而並未提到青花瓷。在十四世紀三十年代時有汪大淵所著「島夷志略」，曾提到作者遠涉南洋時曾有「青白花瓷」之稱。元代中葉起青花瓷即外銷南洋島夷，並延伸至中東人士之欣然接受，而造成了大量的外銷，其造瓷工藝亦在精益見精中，更創新猷，為明初青

花瓷的精美闢出蹊徑。

元代青花瓷無官窯這回事，大量的燒瓷工業，都為外銷及民間用器物而努力。但到了明代，情形就不同了。據「事物紺珠」所提：「永樂、宣德二窯，皆內府燒造，以棕眼甜白為常，以蘇麻離青為飾。」又博物要覽云：「永樂年造壓手杯，中心畫隻獅滾球為上品，鴛鴦心者次之，花心者又次。杯外青花深翠，式樣精妙，若近時仿效，殊無可觀。」又南村隨筆：「明景德鎮所造，永樂尚厚，成化尚薄，宣德青尚淡，嘉靖青尚濃，成青未若宣青，宣彩未若成彩。」對明青花瓷的要點，可以得其大概矣。

青花瓷的顏料據本書前述有外國及本地產二大系，一般說來外國色料高鐵低錳，色澤清亮透明厚青處出現鐵斑。國產色料含低鐵高錳，呈色淡雅，青中含灰色。至於青花瓷的胎土大都屬於一種稱為高嶺土者，色素而白，略

帶青色。若胎土中帶金屬,則燒後泛紅或褐黃。底白晶瑩
如玉,有閃爍若金星者最上。至於釉原料,乃是將鳳尾草
和青白石層層交替,疊在石灰窯中燒成灰,取灰經數度淘
洗後,加入白質細泥(此或即含矽質砂粒,於加熱後即成
一層玻璃體),此項混合即成釉料。中含微量鐵元素,因
帶不同程度青色,到清代這種含青色澤漸減退,至清代末
年,以成無色透明體,釉中氣泡成因,是燒時溫度不夠,
氣體無法溢出,故溫度若低,氣泡越多且密。氣泡使釉質
失透明度而有玉質感,或出現橘皮紋。但到清代後期,氣
泡不再出現的原因。

　　青花瓷飾紋見有用印花方法者,是一種模印再上鈷藍
鉤勒而成。另有一種滿塗青料作底的白色紋飾,即青地白
花,先用青料在胎面紋飾外隙地塗滿青色,以青花琉璃釉
為最多,青色釉面濃厚無紋飾,但在宣德時見有塗青地上
加線繪,到康熙時冰梅紋以青花鉤出梅花。另有所謂滿清
和灑藍二種,前者通體塗以鈷藍,留出些白花雕塑。灑藍
是用青料吹灑於器物上,燒成器後藍色中有片片絮狀白
色,故又稱雪花藍。另再有一種青花,以黃色或其它色料
作底色。先以鈷藍白地高溫燒出,再用色釉填上白地,經
低溫二次燒出。更有一種青花釉上彩,乃青花鉤邊後再加
填彩繪,二次燒出。似乎是鬥彩瓷的濫觴。

　　中國悠久的歷史、遼闊的幅員及博大精深的文化,孕
育出無與倫比,舉世讚歎的「青花瓷」,今得以一賞前人
藝術精華,實乃後輩之福也。

Q-16
Liao Dynasty
About 1000 A.D.

Underglazed Red of Lotus Pond / Baby at Play pattern Plate.
Height over all : 3.3cm. Mouth Dia. : 14cm.
Foot rim Dia. : 6cm.
宋（遼）　釉裡紅蓮塘嬰戲紋盤
總高約：3.3cm.　盤口徑約：14cm.　圈足約：6cm.

K-1
Yuan Dynasty
About 14th Century

Deep Blue Glaze with Lotus Base and Flared Mouth Vase.
Height: about 33.5cm. Mouth Dia.: 10.5cm. Foot rim Dia.: 11.8cm.
元　藍釉蓮座式敞口瓶　高約33.5cm.　口徑10.5cm.　圈足約11.8cm.

Q-23
Yuan Dynasty
About 13ᵗʰ Century

Blue Glaze of Interlocking Flower pattern Jar. With 5 layers of patterns: Brake, 10 parted precious items, Subjective Interlocking Flower, Ancient Coin and 8 parted Lotus petal Cloud.
Height: 16.8cm. Mouth Dia.: 10.4cm. Foot rim Dia.: 8.8cm.
元　青花纏枝花卉紋罐　〈全器分五層繪飾，第一層繪鳳尾草紋，第二層繪10格吉祥紋飾，第三層為主體繪纏枝花卉紋，第四層繪圓方孔錢紋，第五層繪8格蓮瓣雲頭紋。〉
總高約：16.8cm.　口徑約：10.4m.　圈足約：8.8cm.

15

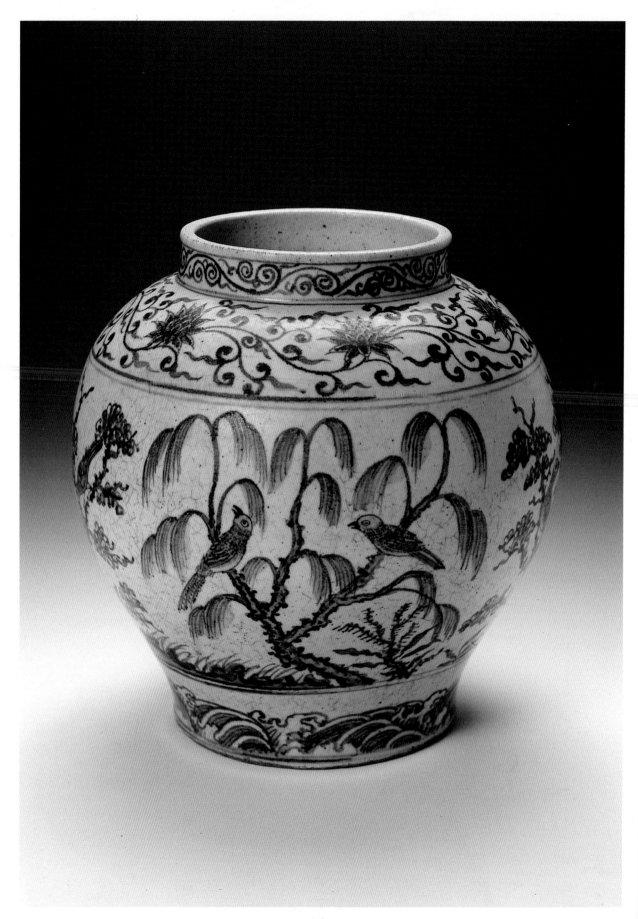

Q-46
Yuan Dynasty
1271 ~ 1368 A.D.

Chingtehcheng Blue Glaze of Interlocking Lily, Flower / Bird and Sea Wave pattern Jar.
Height over all : 24.7cm.　Mouth Dia. : 13.5cm.　Foot rim Dia. : 14.5cm.

A.　Cobalt blue soaked into inner clay with iron spots.
B.　With crackle pales on surface of glaze and soil soak proves obviously of hundred of years.
C.　Picture on body in scroll painting of grasses on upper of shoulder and with lotus on shoulder, birds and willow trees at middle and wave at bottom which reflects typical vogue of Yuan style.
D.　Red color clay appears at base and a nipple nail head at center which represents the method of the production of the period.

Remarks : 1.　Please refer to 1991 ~ 1992 Taiwan Yellow Page.
　　　　 2.　Special Report on Ta Ming Daily News, Sept. 25th, 1992.
　　　　 3.　Please see First Auction Catalog of Sunrise in January, 1995.

元　景德鎮　青花纏枝蕃蓮花鳥浪濤紋罐
總高約：24.7cm.　口徑約：13.5cm.　圈足約：14.5cm.
特徵：
　　A.　蘇麻離青鐵斑自然下沉，浸咬入胎骨內層。(非僅限於釉面)
　　B.　釉面層有細微開片，土浸完全溶入開片中，非歷經數百年時間土浸無法浸入。
　　C.　本件藏品之畫工，不論是肩部纏枝蕃蓮紋，口部之捲草紋，主題之喜上眉梢、喜上柳枝、底部之海浪紋，皆數當時代元人之習慣畫工。
　　D.　罐底之胎土屬自然之火紅色，玄紋底，胎底正中有乳釘狀之突出，皆數當時代工匠之作工習慣，可做為重要之斷代依據。
　註：1.　本件曾刊載於1991 ~ 1992年版 Taiwan Yellow Pages 年刊
　　　 2.　本件曾於1992年9月25日在大明報收藏版專文介紹。
　　　 3.　本件曾於1995年元月份於臺灣東業拍賣公司展出拍賣並拍出。(可參考1995年元月東業拍賣專刊 P.10)

B-1
Yuan Dynasty
About 13/14th Century

Blue Glaze with double ears design of octagonal medallion shaped Jar.
Height about: 39.6cm.   Mouth Dia.: 12.2cm.   Foot rim Dia.: 16.3cm.
元　青花雙獅耳八角形八面開光罐
高約39.6cm.　口徑約12.2cm.　底徑約16.3cm.

Q-11
Yuan Dynasty
About 13th Century

Underglazed Red of Banana Leaves / 3 Winter Friends pattern Garlic Head Vase. With 5 layers of pattern: Chrysanthemum and Interlocking Branches, Triangular Banana Leaves, Rolled Grass, Pine, Bamboo & Plum and Lotus petal / Cloud.
Height over all: 28.9cm. Mouth Dia.: 4.2cm. Foot rim Dia.: 9.7cm.
元 釉裡紅蕉葉歲寒三友蒜頭瓶 〈全器分五層繪飾，第一層繪菊花纏枝紋，第二層繪三角蕉葉紋，第三層繪捲草紋，第四層繪松、竹、梅，第五層繪蓮瓣雲頭紋。〉 總高約：28.9cm. 口徑約：4.2cm. 圈足約：9.7cm.

B-2
Yuan Dynasty
About 14th Century

Blue Glaze of rhombus shape edge mouth and Lotus pond/Bird pattern Plate.
Mouth Dia.： 50.8cm.　Foot rim Dia.： 31.3cm.
元　青花菱花口荷塘水禽紋盤　口徑50.8cm　圈足31.3cm.

D-1
Yuan Dynasty
About 13ᵗʰ Century

Blue Glaze of Phoenix / Flower Design Plate in rhombus shaped mouth edge Plate.   With inner 3 layers of designs :
Rolled Grass, Interlocking Lily and subjective Phoenix / Flower also with Peony & Interlocking branches pattern on
outside edge.
Mouth Dia. : 44cm.   Height : 7.2cm.   Foot rim Dia. : 29cm.
元　菱花口邊青花鳳凰花卉紋盤　〈盤內繪飾三層，第一層繪捲草紋，第二層繪纏枝蕃蓮紋，第三層為主圖案繪鳳凰花卉紋，盤外
沿繪纏枝牡丹紋〉
口徑約44cm.　總高約7.2cm.　圈足約29cm.

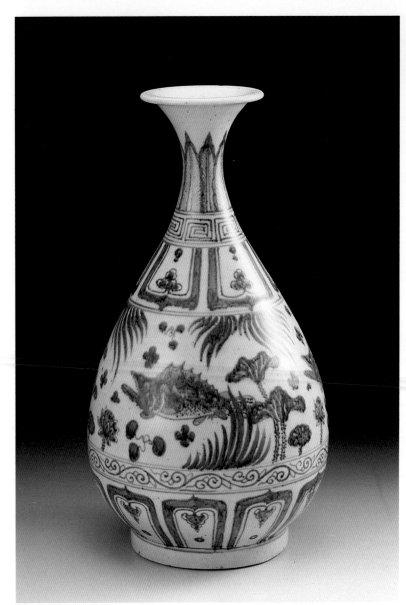
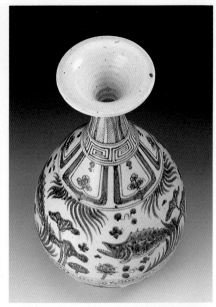
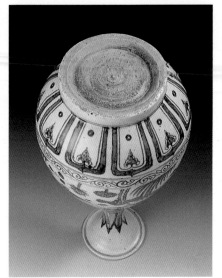

D-2
Yuan Dynasty
About 13ᵗʰ Century

Blue Glaze of Fish Swimming in Lotus Pond pattern Pear shaped Vase. With design of 6 layers: Banana Leaves, Moslem Characters, Cloud / Fungus, Subjective Fish swimming in lotus pond and Rolled Grass with Ru Yi.
Height over all: 34.8cm. Mouth Dia.: 9.5cm. Foot rim Dia.: 12.5cm.
元　青花蓮塘游魚玉壺春瓶　〈瓶身總體分六層繪飾，第一層繪蕉葉紋，第二層繪回紋連續圖，第三層繪朵雲形靈芝，第四層繪主圖蓮塘游魚，第五層繪捲草紋，第六層繪如意形圖飾〉
總高約34.8cm.　口徑約9.5cm.　圈足約12.5cm.

Q-43
Yuan Dynasty
About 13ᵗʰ Century

Blue Glaze of 3 Winter Friends pattern Jar. With 4 layers of pattern: Square, Rolled Grass, Subjective of Pine, Bamboo, Plum and Lotus petals / Cloud in 9 squares.
Height over all: 17.8cm. Mouth Dia.: 13.6cm. Foot rim Dia.: 13.1cm.
元　青花歲寒三友罐　〈全器分四層繪飾，第一層繪方勝紋，第二層繪捲草紋，第三層為主體繪松、竹、梅，第四層繪9格蓮瓣朵雲紋。〉
總高約：17.8cm.　口徑約：13.6cm.　圈足約：13.1cm.

23

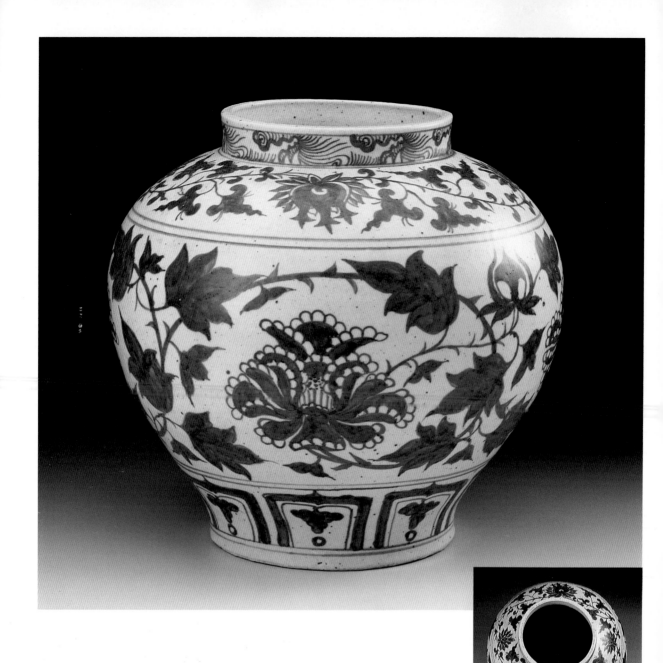

D-3
Yuan Dynasty
About 13th Century

Blue Glaze of Peony / Interlocking Flowers designed Jar.　With 4 layers of
patterns： Sea Wave, Interlocking branches & Pomegranate Flower with
subjective Peony / Cloud pattern.
Height over all： 26.3cm.　Mouth Dia.： 14.5cm.　Foot rim Dia.：15.5cm.
元　青花牡丹纏枝花卉罐　〈罐身總體分四層繪飾，第一層繪海浪紋，第二層繪纏枝
蕃蓮石榴花卉紋，第三層繪主圖牡丹纏枝花卉紋，第四層繪朵雲紋〉
總高約26.3cm.　口徑約14.5cm.　圈足約15.5cm.

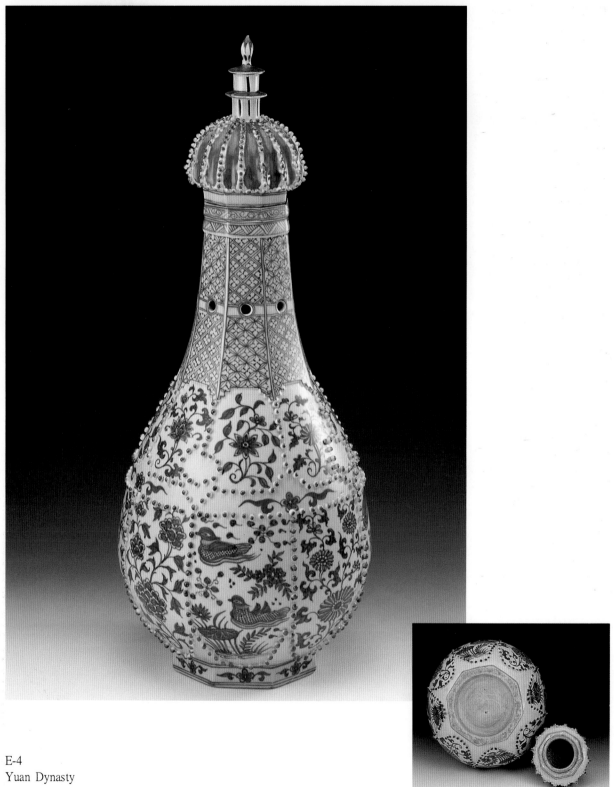

E-4
Yuan Dynasty
About 13th Century

Blue Glaze of octagonal shape with Flower/ Mandarin Duck in pond inside a necklaced frame pattern Vase with cover.
Height: 59cm.　Mouth Dia.: 8cm.　Foot rim Dia.: 13.8cm.
元　青花八角蓮塘鴛鴦花卉瓔珞紋帶蓋瓶　〈瓶身分八層繪製〉
總高約59cm.　瓶口徑約8cm.　底徑約13.8cm.

Q-56
Yuan Dynasty
About 14th Century

Blue Glaze of Immortal Figure pattern pear shaped vase.
Mouth Dia. about：5cm. Height about：35cm.
元　青花仙道人物圖玉壺春瓶　口徑約：5cm.　高約：35cm.

Q-28
Yuan Dynasty
About 13th Century

Blue Glaze of Lotus Pond / Bird pattern Rhombus shaped Edge Plate. With 3 layers of pattern inside plate: Squares design, Interlocking Flowers and Subjective Lotus Pond / Bird. On outer edge with Interlocking Flowers pattern.
Height: 7.3cm. Mouth Dia.: 37.2cm. Foot rim Dia.: 23.6cm.
元　青花蓮塘水禽紋棱口盤　〈盤內沿分三層繪飾，第一層口沿部份繪方勝紋，第二層繪纏枝花卉紋，第三層為主體繪蓮塘水禽紋；盤外沿繪纏枝花卉紋。〉
總高約：7.3cm.　盤口徑約：37.2cm.　圈足約：23.6cm.

H-4
Yuan Dynasty
About 13ᵗʰ Century

Blue Glaze of Interlocking Peony pattern Mei Ping. With 6 layers of patterns: Rolled Grass, Ru Yi on shoulder and 4 direction medallion of Phoenix, Rolled Grass then subjective pattern of Interlocking Peony, coins lining and cloud near foot.　Height: 51cm.　Mouth Dia.: 6cm.　Foot rim Dia.: 19.4cm.

元　青花牡丹纏枝紋梅瓶　〈瓶身總體分六層繪飾，第一層繪捲草紋，第二層瓶肩部繪如意開光鳳紋圖四面，第三層繪捲草紋，第四層主體繪牡丹纏枝紋，第五層繪開孔錢紋，第六層足部繪朵雲紋飾〉
總高約51cm.　口徑約6cm.　圈足約19.4cm.

Q-53
Yuan Dynasty
About 13th Century

Blue Glaze of Figure Story Pear shaped Vase.
Height: 27.5cm.   Mouth Dia.: 9cm.   Foot rim Dia.: 8.4cm.
元　青花人物故事玉壺春瓶
總高約：27.5cm.　口徑約：9cm.　圈足約：8.4cm.

Q-1
Yuan Dynasty
About 14th Century

Blue Glaze of Lotus Pond / Flower pattern Plate. With 3 layers of pattern: Rolled Grass, Interlocking Lily and Subjective Lotus Pond / Flower. Also decorated with 16 medallion Ruyi on outer edge.
Mouth Dia.: 38.7cm. Height over all: 5.7cm. Foot rim Dia.: 24.4cm.
元　青花蓮塘花卉紋棱口盤　〈盤內沿正面分三層繪飾，第一層繪捲草紋，第二層繪蕃蓮紋，第三層主圖繪飾蓮塘花卉紋，盤外沿繪16格朵雲如意紋飾〉
口徑：38.7cm.　總高約：5.7cm.　圈足約：24.4cm.

Q-54
Yuan Dynasty
About 13th Century

Blue Glaze of Lotus Pond / Bird and Interlocking Lily pattern Mei Ping.
Height : 28.5cm.　Mouth Dia. : 3.5cm.　Foot rim Dia. : 8.7cm.
元　青花蓮塘水禽纏枝蕃蓮紋梅瓶
總高約：28.5cm.　口徑約：3.5cm.　圈足約：8.7cm.

Q-17
Yuan ～ Ming Dynasties
About 14ᵗʰ Century

Blue Glaze Underglazed Red of Interlocking Branches / Flower Large Bowl. With 3 layers of pattern: Rolled Grass,
Subjective Interlocking Branches / Flower and Lotus petals.
Height over all: 15.6cm.   Mouth Dia.: 30.4cm.   Foot rim Dia.: 16cm.
元～明　青花釉裡紅纏枝花卉紋大碗　〈全器外沿分三層繪飾，第一層繪捲草紋，第二層繪纏枝花卉紋，第三層繪蓮瓣紋。〉
總高約：15.6cm.　盤口徑約：30.4cm.　圈足約：16cm.

Q-32
Yuan ～ Ming Dynasties
About 13ᵗʰ Century

Blue Glaze of Winter 3 Friends and Banana Leaves pattern Stem Bowl.
Height: 8.2cm.　Mouth Dia.: 11.3cm.　Foot rim Dia.: 5.1cm.
元～明　青花歲寒三友蕉葉紋高足碗
總高約：8.2cm.　口徑約：11.3cm.　底徑約：5.1cm.

M-1
Yuan to Ming Dynasties
About 14th Century

Blue Glaze of Bundle Lotus pattern Plate.   With 3 layers of pattern in inner：Rolled Grass, Interlocking Flower,
Subjective Bundle Lotus.   Also with 3 layers at outer edge：Rolled Grass, Interlocking Flowers and spiral decorated
design.
Mouth Dia.：35.7cm.   Height：7cm.   Foot rim Dia.：23.4cm.
元～明　青花把蓮紋盤　〈盤內分三層繪飾，第一層繪捲草紋，第二層繪纏枝花卉紋，第三層為主體繪把蓮圖飾。盤外沿亦分三層
繪飾，第一層繪飾捲草紋，第二層繪飾纏枝花卉紋，第三層繪迴紋裝飾。〉
口徑約35.7cm.　總高約7cm.　圈足約23.4cm.

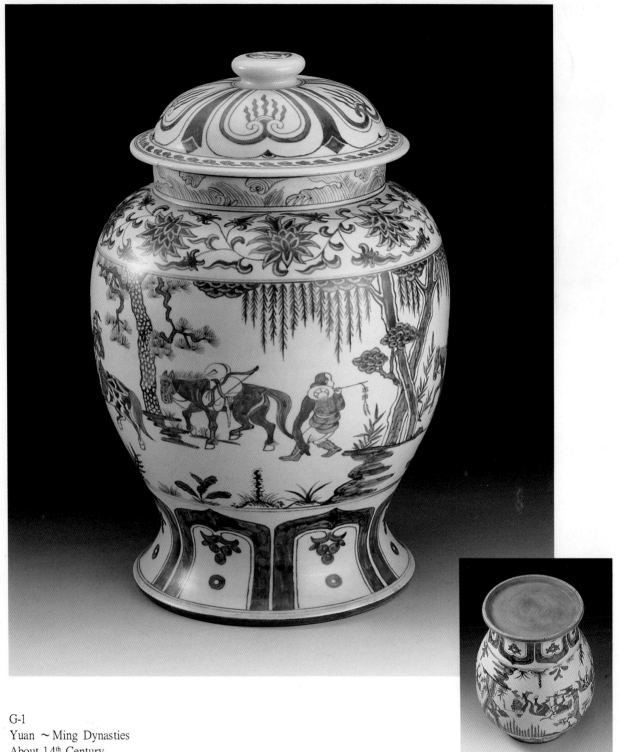

G-1
Yuan ～ Ming Dynasties
About 14ᵗʰ Century

Blue Glaze of Journey of Han Beauty with Interlocking Lily pattern Jar with cover. With 7 layers of pattern: Pattern of Crane on cover, Cloud Flame, Ruyi / Cloud, Sea Wave on mouth edge, Interlocking Lily and then Subjective Journey of Han Beauty with 7 Lotus petals near foot.
Height over all: 35.5cm. Mouth Dia.: 15.5cm. Foot rim Dia.: 19cm.
元～明　青花纏枝蕃蓮昭君出塞帶蓋罐　〈罐身帶蓋總體分七層繪飾，第一層蓋紐繪鶴鳥紋，第二層火雲頭紋，第三層如意雲紋，第四層罐口沿繪海浪紋，第五層繪纏枝蕃蓮紋，第六層為主體繪昭君出塞，第七層繪七格蓮瓣紋〉
總高約：35.5cm. 口徑約：15.5cm. 圈足約：19cm.

B-3
Yuan to Early Ming Dynasties
About 14th Century

Underglazed Red ground with white embossed Flower design Flared Mouth Bowl.
Height over all: 25cm.　Mouth Dia.: 56.7cm.　Foot rim Dia.: 27.4cm.
元～明初　釉裡紅底白釉堆花敞口大碗
總高約25cm.　口徑約56.7cm.　圈足約27.4cm.

Q-24
Yuan ～Ming Dynasties
About 14th Century

Blue Glaze of 3 Winter Friends pattern Mei Ping. With 6 layers of pattern: Banana Leaves, Rolled Grass, 8 precious items, Subjective Pine, Bamboo & Plum, Ancient Coin and Lotus petals with cloud.
Height: 16cm. Mouth Dia.: 2.5cm. Foot rim Dia.: 5cm.
元～明　青花歲寒三友梅瓶　〈全器分六層繪飾，第一層繪蕉葉紋，第二層繪捲草紋，第三層繪8吉祥紋，第四層為主題繪松、竹、梅，第五層繪圓方孔錢紋，第六層繪蓮瓣雲頭紋。〉
總高約：16cm.　瓶口徑約：2.5m.　圈足約：5cm.

37

Q-18
Yuan ～ Ming Dynasties
About 13ᵗʰ Century

Blue Glaze of Cloud / Dragon pattern Jar.　With 5 layers of pattern：Rolled Grass, Interlocking Branch / Flower, Subjective Cloud / Double Dragon, Rolled Grass and Lotus Petal / Cloud.
Height over all：17cm.　Mouth Dia.：13.1cm.　Foot rim Dia.：14.2cm.
元～明　青花朵雲龍紋罐　〔全器分五層繪飾，第一層繪捲草紋，第二層繪纏枝花卉紋，第三層為主體繪朵雲雙龍紋，第四層繪捲草紋，第五層繪蓮瓣朵雲紋。〕　總高約：17cm.　口徑約：13.1cm.　圈足約：14.2cm.

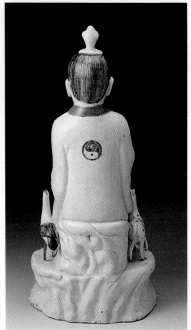

Q-37
Yuan ～Ming Dynasties
About 14th Century

Blue Glaze / Underglazed Red of Immortal Chang Tsun Tse. With pattern of Dear / Crane and Ta Chi Symbol
representing "Chang Tsun Tse also Known as Chiu Tsu Chi". Height over all：34.4cm.
元～明　青花釉裡紅長春子造像　〈鹿、鶴亦謂長春，人物之背面繪道教之圖徽太極圖，故本尊造像應是道教重要人物之一『丘處
機』。〉　總高約：34.4cm.

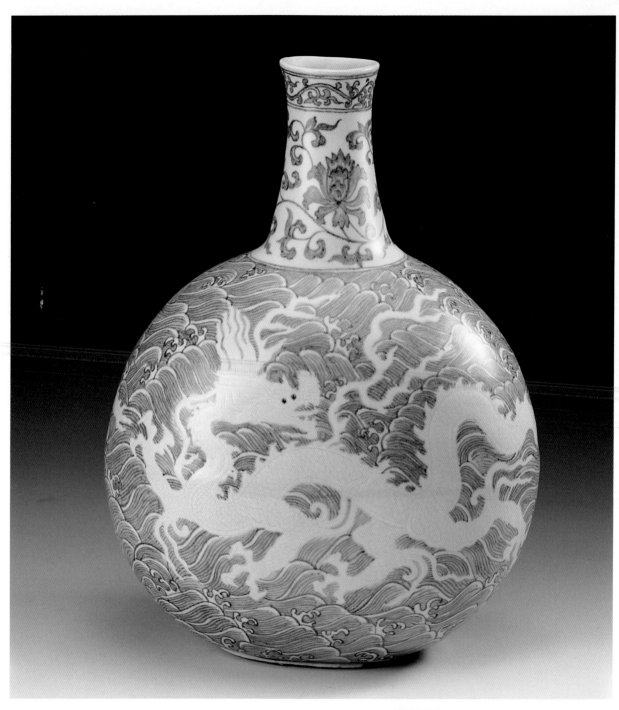

Q-52
Early Ming Dynasty
About 14th Century

Blue Glaze of White Ground Dragon in Sea Semi Circular
Globular Vase.
Height: 48.7cm.　Mouth Dia.: 8cm.　Foot rim Dia.: 17cm.
明早期　青花白花底遊龍出海扁圓天球瓶
總高約：48.7cm.　口徑約：8cm.　圈足約：17cm.

40

O-2
Early Ming Dynasty
About early 14ᵗʰ Century

Blue Glaze of veiled carving Sea Wave/ Dragon pattern Jar.
(with Banana Leaves design on shoulder and near foot)
Height over all : 31.9cm.　Mouth Dia. : 14.4cm.　Foot rim Dia. : 20.2cm.
明　早期青花暗刻海浪龍紋罐　〈罐肩及近圈足處繪飾蕉葉紋〉
總高約31.9cm.　口徑約14.4cm　圈足約20.2cm.

E-5
Early Ming Dynasty
About 14ᵗʰ Century

Blue Glaze of Floral design of chrysanthemum spray and rolled grass lining of semi-coin. Also peony pattern at center of bowl with base tray which decorated with coins lining, peony, cloud and banana leaves.
Height over all: 10.9cm.　Height of Bowl: 5.1cm.　Mouth Dia. of Bowl: 11.1cm.
Foot rim Dia. of Bowl: 4.3cm.　Height of tray: 6.7cm.　Dia.: 5.2cm.
明初　青花花卉紋盞托暨碗　〈碗心繪牡丹，碗內口沿繪捲草紋，碗外口沿繪半圓錢連續紋，碗外沿身繪菊花折枝紋〉
《盞托第一層繪錢紋連續紋，盞托第二層繪牡丹紋，第三層繪朵雲，第四層繪蕉葉》
總高約10.9cm.　碗高約5.1cm.　碗口徑約11.1cm.　碗圈足約4.3cm.
盞托部總高約6.7cm.　盞托底徑約5.2cm.

D-5
Early Ming Dynasty
About 14ᵗʰ Century

Blue Glaze of Four Seasons Flower and Garden Scenic designed Plate. With Four Seasons Flower and Garden & Stone at inner bottom and rolled Grass / 4 seasons Flower at outside edge on mouth.
Mouth Dia.: 41.6cm. Height over all: 7.6cm. Foot rim Dia.: 27cm.
明早期 青花四季花卉庭園山石盤 〈盤內繪四季花卉庭園山石，外沿繪捲草紋及四季花卉圖〉
口徑約41.6cm. 總高約7.6cm. 圈足約27cm.

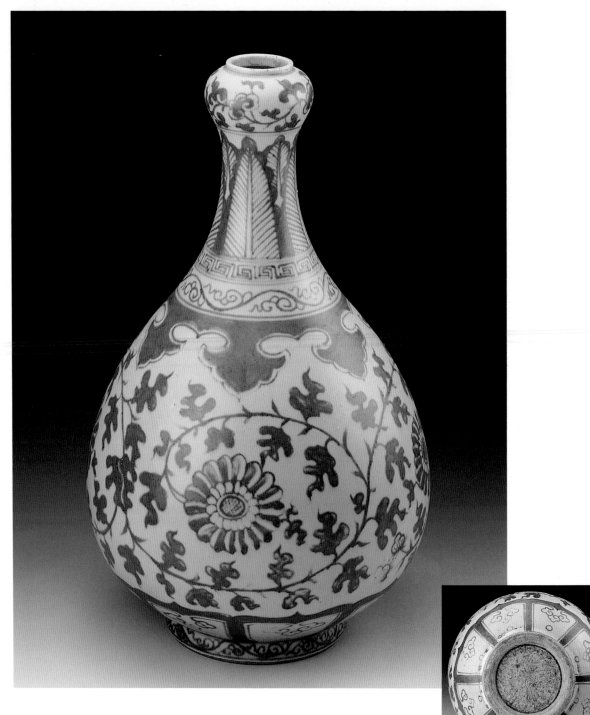

C-1
Early Ming Dynasty
About 14th Century

Underglazed Red of Chrysanthemum / Interlocking Branches Garlick shaped Vase. With 8 layers of Rolled Grass / Flower, Banana Leaves, Moslem Characters, Rolled Grass, Ru Yi, Subjective Chrysanthemum / interlocking branches, Cloud and Rolled Grass patterns.
Height over all : 37cm. Mouth Dia. about : 4.2cm. Foot rim Dia. : 11.7cm.
明初　釉裡紅菊花纏枝紋蒜頭瓶　〈瓶身總體分八層繪飾，第一層繪捲草花卉紋，第二層繪蕉葉紋，第三層繪回紋連續圖案，第四層繪捲草紋，第五層繪如意紋，第六層為主圖繪菊花纏枝紋，第七層繪朵雲紋，第八層繪捲草紋〉
總高約37cm.　口徑約4.2cm.　圈足約11.7cm.

Q-14
Middle Ming Dynasty
About 14ᵗʰ Century

Blue Glaze of Interlocking Lily pattern Crock.
Height: 33.5cm. Mouth Dia.: 25.7cm. Base Dia: 27.3cm.
明中早期　青花纏枝蕃蓮紋缸
總高約：33.5cm.　口徑約：25.7cm.　底徑約：27.3cm.

Q-20
Early ∼ Middle Ming Dynasty
About 14th Century

Blue Glaze of 4 Season Flower pattern Candle Stay in pair.
Height in average: 26.5cm.　Base Dia.: 18.2cm.
明中早期　青花四季花卉燭臺壹對　平均總高：26.5cm.　底徑：18.2cm.

Q-30
Early to Middle Ming Dynasties
About 15ᵗʰ Century

Blue Glaze of Interlocking Lily with Cloud / Dragon / Phoenix pattern Garlic Head shaped Vase. With 6 layers of
pattern : Rolled Grass, Ruyi medallion with Cloud / Dragon / Phoenix, Interlocking Lily, Rolled Grass, Subjective
Cloud / Dragon / Phoenix and 16 parted Lotus petals and Cloud.
Height : 60cm. Mouth Dia. : 9.8cm. Foot rim Dia. : 19.3cm.
明中早期 青花纏枝蕃蓮朵雲龍鳳紋蒜頭瓶 〈瓶身總體分六層繪飾，第一層繪捲草紋，第二層繪如意開光朵雲龍鳳紋，第三層繪
纏枝蕃蓮紋，第四層繪捲草紋，第五層為主體繪朵雲龍鳳紋飾，第六層繪16格蓮瓣雲頭紋飾。〉
總高約：60cm. 瓶口徑約：9.8cm. 圈足約：19.3cm.

Q-34
Ming Dynasty
About 15th Century

Underglazed Red of Interlocking Lily pattern in Sycee Shape Handle Pot.
Height: 21.5cm. Mouth Dia.: 2.6cm.
明　釉裡紅纏枝蕃蓮元寶形執壺
平均總高約：21.5cm.　入水口徑約：2.6cm.

P-1
Ming Dynasty
About 15th Century

Underglazed Red Stem Foot Plate. In pattern of Double Carp and Water Weed at center of Plate.
Height over all : 9cm. Dia. About : 18cm. Foot rim Dia. : 8.3cm.
明　釉裡紅高足盤　〈盤心繪雙金魚藻紋飾〉
總高約：9cm.　直徑約：18cm.　底徑約：8.3cm.

E-3
Ming Dynasty
About 15th Century

Blue Glaze Flask / Double Gourd shape double ears and sash pattern Vase.
Height: 30cm.　Mouth Dia.: 3.3cm.　Foot rim size: 9 × 6cm.
明　青花扁圓葫蘆形雙耳綬帶瓶
總高約30cm.　口徑約3.3cm.　底徑約9cm.×6cm.

50

A-4
Ming Dynasty
About 15ᵗʰ Century

Blue Glaze of Phoenix Head design Mei Ping. (Remark： Refer to SUNRISE 4ᵗʰ auction Page 131.)
Height over all： 34.5cm.　Foot rim Dia.： 10.7cm.
明　青花鳳首瓶　總高約34.5cm.　圈足約10.7cm.

A-2
Ming Dynasty
About 16th Century

Blue Glaze of Peony / Interlocking Branches Military Ewer.
Height over all : 15cm.   Foot rim Dia. : 7cm.
明　青花牡丹纏枝紋軍持瓶　總高約15cm.　圈足約7cm.

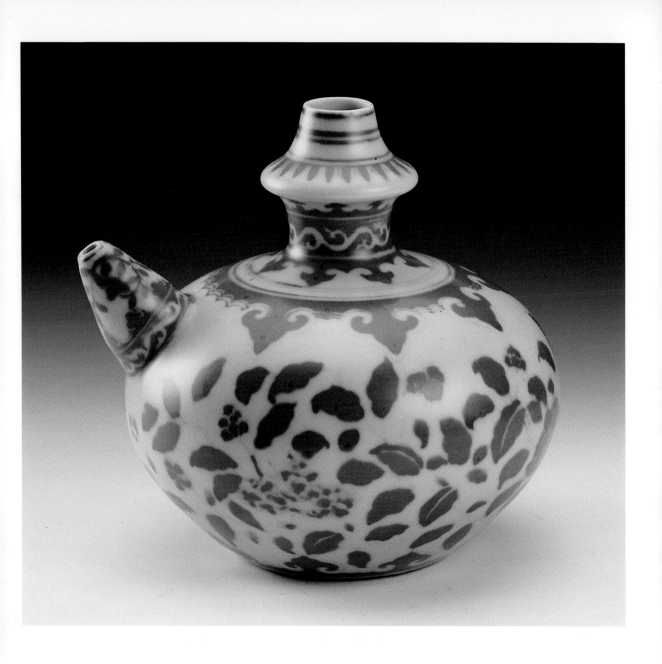

A-3
Ming Dynasty
About 16th Century

Underglazed Red of Peony / spray branches pattern Military Ewer.
Height over all: 15cm.   Foot rim Dia.: 6.9cm.
明　釉裡紅牡丹折枝紋軍持瓶　總高約15cm.　圈足約6.9cm.

H-3
Ming Dynasty
Era of Hsien Teh   (1430)

Blue Glaze of Interlocking Grape pattern Bowl.   Marked with : "Ta Ming Hsien Teh Nien Tse" 6 orthodox characters in blue double circle.   Inner design of Rolled Grass / 10 Fungus, design of Peach of Longevity at center.   With Interlocking Grape outer and Rolled Grass on foot rim.
Mouth Dia. : 28.4cm.   Height : 12.4cm.   Foot rim Dia. : 12.7cm.
明　青花纏枝葡萄紋碗　落大明宣德年製六字楷書青花雙圈款　〈碗內邊沿飾捲草靈芝紋十朵，內底繪青花壽桃，碗外沿繪飾纏枝葡萄紋，圈足處繪捲草紋〉
口徑約28.4cm.　總高約12.4cm.　圈足約12.7cm.

54

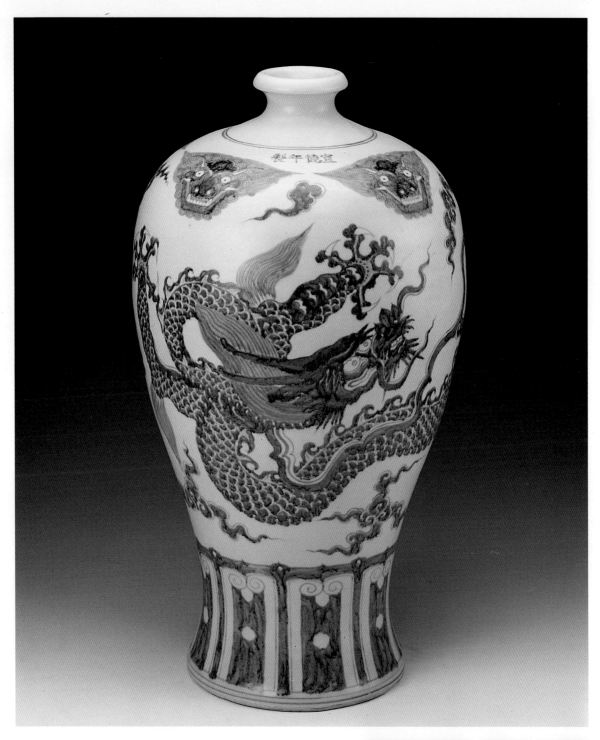

I-1
Ming Dynasty
Era of Hsien Teh (1430)

Blue Glaze of Cloud / Dragon pattern Mei Ping.
Marked with " Hsien Teh Nien Tse" 4 orthodox character on shoulder.
Height: 50cm.　Mouth Dia.: 7cm.　Foot rim Dia.: 18.5cm.
明　青花朵雲龍紋梅瓶　瓶肩落宣德年製四字楷書款
總高約50cm.　口徑約7cm.　圈足約18.5cm.

Q-55
Ming Dynasty, Era of Hsien Teh
About 1430 A.D.

Blue Glaze of Rolled Grass pattern Jar with cover.
Height with cover: 15cm.　Mouth Dia.: 10.3cm.　Foot rim Dia.: 9.6cm.
明宣德　青花捲草紋帶蓋罐
帶蓋總高約：15cm.　口徑約：10.3cm.　圈足約：9.6cm.

F-1
Ming Dynasty
Era of Hsien Teh (1430)

Blue Glaze of Dragon / Interlocking Lily design in Rhombus shaped Edge Plate. With 3 layers of patterns: Sea Wave, Double Dragon & Interlocking branches Lily, subjective Dragon & Interlocking branches Lily, also of interlocking branches Lily at outside of edge.
Height: 14cm. Mouth Dia.: 79cm. Foot rim Dia.: 49cm.
明宣德　青花菱花口邊龍紋纏枝蕃蓮盤　〈盤內沿分三層繪飾，第一層繪海浪紋，第二層繪雙龍纏枝蕃蓮，第三層主體繪龍紋纏枝蕃蓮，盤外沿繪雙龍纏枝蕃蓮紋〉　總高約14cm.　口徑約79cm.　圈足約49cm.

Q-39
Ming Dynasty, Era of Cheng Hua
About 1470 A.D.

Blue Glaze of Pine, Bamboo, Plum, Chrysanthemum and Banana Leaves pattern Jar.　Marked with single character：
"TIEN".　With 4 layers of pattern： Squares, Banana Leaves, Subjective Pine, Bamboo Plum, Chrysanthemum and
Banana Leaves with Stone & Tree parted Lotus petals / Cloud.
Height： 26.1cm.　Mouth Dia.： 15.5cm.　Foot rim Dia.： 18.2cm.
明成化　青花松、竹、梅、菊，山石、蕉樹紋罐　罐底落楷書「天」字款　〈罐身總體分四層繪飾，第一層繪方勝紋，第二層繪蕉
葉紋，第三層為罐身主體繪松、竹、梅、菊，山石、蕉樹紋，第四層繪12格蓮瓣朵雲紋。〉
總高約：26.1cm.　口徑約：15.5cm.　圈足約：18.2cm.

H-2
Ming Dynasty
Era of Cheng Hua   (1470)

Blue Glaze of Lotus Pond / Fish Weed pattern Flared Mouth Bowl.   Marked with : "Ta Ming Cheng Hua Nien Tse"
6 orthodox characters in blue double circle both inner / outer with Lotus Pond / Fish Weed design.
Mouth Dia. : 22cm.   Height : 10.8ccm.   Foot rim Dia. : 9.9cm.
明　青花蓮塘魚藻紋敞口碗　落大明成化年製六字楷書青花雙圈款　〈碗內沿底繪蓮塘魚藻圖，碗外沿繪青花蓮塘魚藻紋〉
口徑22cm.　總高約10.8cm.　圈足約9.9cm.

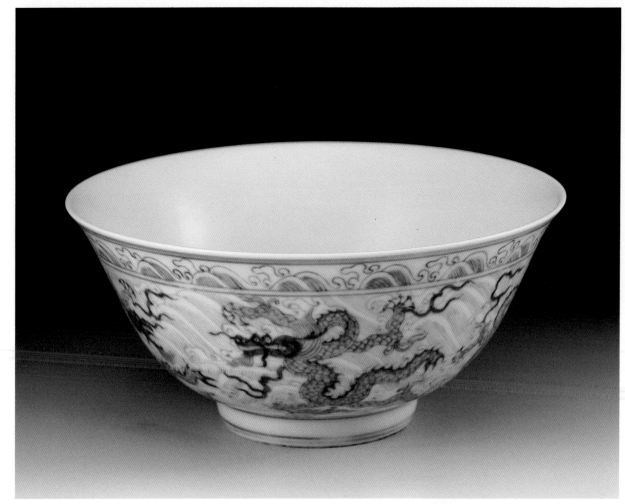

H-1
Ming Dynasty
Era of Cheng Hua (1470)

Blue Glaze of Dragon / Sea Wave pattern Bowl. Marked with : "Ta Ming Cheng Hua Nien Tse" 6 orthodox characters in blue double circle. 〈Subjective pattern of 5 tail Blue Dragon and Sea Wave〉.
Mouth Dia.: 17.5cm. Height: 8.1cm. Foot rim Dia.: 6.9cm.
明　青花龍紋浪濤碗　落大明成化年製六字楷書青花雙圈款　〈碗身主體繪五尾青花龍，配以浪濤紋飾〉
口徑17.5cm.　總高約8.1cm.　圈足約6.9cm.

Q-49
Ming Dynasty, Era of Hung Tsu
About 1500 A.D.

Blue Glaze of Floral Edge and Pine / Crane pattern Plate.
Height: 5.4cm.　Mouth Dia.: 28cm.　Foot rim Dia.: 16.8cm.
明弘治　青花棱花邊松鶴圖紋盤
總高約：5.4cm.　口徑約：28cm.　圈足約：16.8cm.

Q-2
Ming Dynasty, Era of Chia Jing
About 15th Century

Blue Glaze of Five Dragons / Cloud pattern Plate. Marked with " Ta Ming Chia Jing Nien Tse" of blue orthodox characters. With 2 layers inside plate : 4 Dragons / Cloud and Subjective 1 Dragon / Cloud. On outer surface with 3 layers : in lined triangle pattern, lined Ruyi and small Lotus petal pattern.
☆The piece was taken by Allied Army during Boxer's Rebellion in 1900 and believed it was bought from Moscow.
Mouth Dia. : 67.5cm. Height over all : 10.5cm. Foot rim Dia. : 48cm.
明嘉靖　青花五龍朵雲紋盤　盤口沿落大明嘉靖年製六字青花楷書款
☆本件青花盤為清末英法聯軍攻入北京圓明園中運回歐洲，今收藏者由莫斯科購回。　〈盤內沿正面分兩層繪飾，第一層繪四龍朵雲紋，第二層為主體繪飾朵雲龍紋一隻。〉〈盤外沿分三層繪飾，第一層繪三角連續圖紋，第二層繪如意雲紋連續圖，第三層繪小蓮瓣連續圖紋〉　※本件由莫斯科購回之證明文件尚保留於收藏家手中備查。
口徑約：67.5cm.　總高約：10.5cm.　圈足約：48cm.

Q-48
Ming Dynasty
About 15th Century

Blue Glaze with double phoenix pattern plate of folded rim.
Height over all : 38cm. Mouth Dia. : 25.8cm. Base Dia. : 22.4cm.
-Please refer to SUNRISE 4th Auction Catalog Page. 133.-
明中期　青花雙鳳折沿盤
總高約：38cm.　口徑約：25.8cm.　底徑約：22.4cm.

Q-47
Middle of Ming Dynasty
About 15th Century

Blue Glaze of Interlocking Lily and 8 Precious Items pattern Large Crock.
Height： 20cm.　Mouth Dia.： 48.7cm.　Foot rim Dia.： 39.3cm.
明中期　青花纏枝蕃蓮八寶紋大缸
總高約：20cm.　口徑約：48.7cm.　底徑約：39.3cm.

Q-31
Middle of Ming Dynasty
About 16th Century

Blue Glaze of Cloud / 9 Dragon pattern Long Neck Vase.
Height: 49.2cm. Mouth Dia.: 3.7cm. Foot rim Dia.: 9.4cm.
明中期　青花朵雲九龍紋長頸瓶
總高約：49.2cm.　口徑約：3.7cm.　圈足約：9.4cm.

Q-13
Middle of Ming Dynasty
About 15th Century

Blue Glaze of Open Design in Phoenix pattern Jar.
Height over all : 18.8cm. Mouth Dia. : 22.5cm. Foot rim Dia. : 12.7cm.
明中期　青花鳳鳥穿花紋罐
總高約：18.8cm.　口徑約：22.5cm.　底徑約：12.7cm.

Q-5
Middle of Ming Dynasty
About 15th Century

Blue Glaze of Flower pattern 8 petal designed Bowl. With Chrysanthemum pattern at center and 2 layers of outer
pattern: Rolled Grass and 4 Season Flowers.
Height over all: 14.5cm. Mouth Dia.: 29.5cm. Foot rim Dia.: 13cm.
明中期 青花花卉紋八瓣碗 〔碗心繪菊花紋，碗外沿分二層繪飾，第一層繪捲草紋，第二層繪四季花卉紋〕
總高約：14.5cm. 口徑約：29.5cm. 圈足約：13cm.

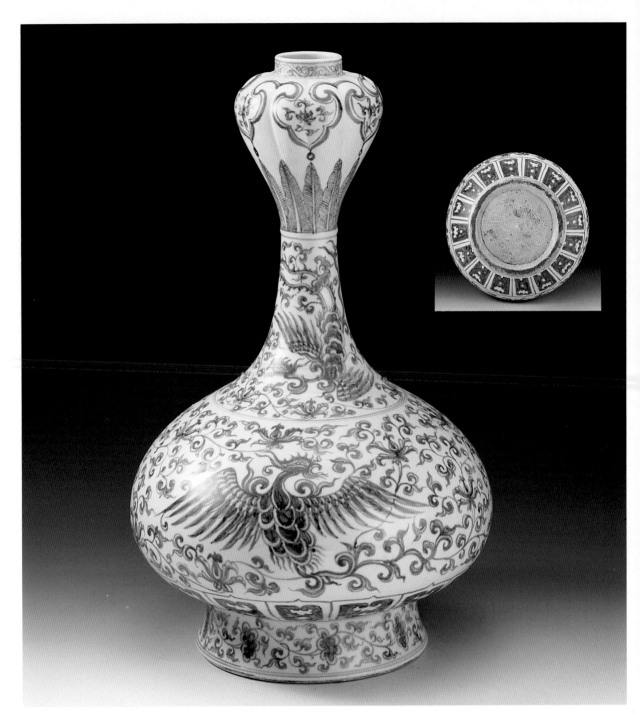

Q-3
Middle Ming Dynasty
About 15th Century

Blue Glaze of Banana Leaf / Flower and Phoenix pattern with Garlick Head shape Vase. With 7 layers of pattern: Rolled Grass, Ruyi and Flower, Banana Leaves and Subjective Interlocking Phoenix as 4th / 5th layer, then 16 white grounded Cloud / Lotus petals and interlocking Flower pattern.
Height over all : 44.8cm. Mouth Dia.: 5cm. Foot rim Dia.: 18cm.
明中期　青花蕉葉花卉鳳鳥紋蒜頭瓶　〈瓶身總體分七層繪飾，第一層為捲草紋飾，第二層如意花卉紋，第三層為蕉葉，第四層第五層為主體繪飾纏枝鳳鳥紋，第六層為16格留白花底朵雲蓮瓣，第七層為纏枝花卉紋。〉
總高約：44.8cm.　口徑約：5cm.　圈足約：18cm.

Q-41
Middle of Ming Dynasty
About 15ᵗʰ Century

Blue Glaze of Phoenix / Spiral Flower pattern Handle Pot with cover.
Height over all： 23cm.　Foot rim Dia.： 7cm.
明中期　青花鳳鳥折枝花卉紋帶蓋執壺　帶蓋總高約：23cm.　圈足約：7cm.

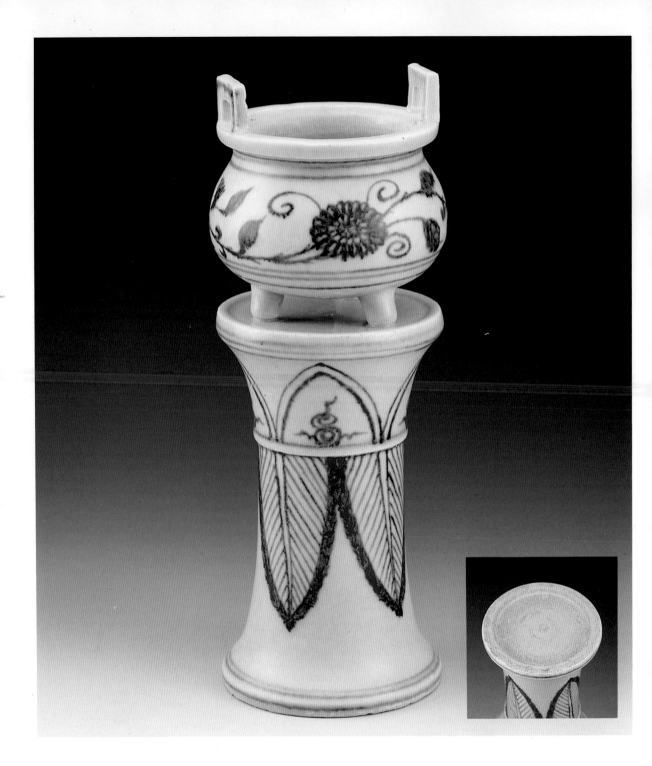

Q-42
Middle of Ming Dynasty
About 15ᵗʰ Century

Blue Glaze of Double Ears and Tri - foot design Incense Burner with stand.　With 3 layers of pattern：Subjective
Interlocking Branches / Chrysanthemum, 4 parted Lotus petals and Banana Leaves.
Height over all：23.8cm.　Dia. of stand：9.7cm.
明中期　青花雙耳三足帶座香爐　〈全器分三層繪飾，第一層香爐主體繪菊花折枝紋，第二層為座身繪４格蓮瓣紋，第三層繪蕉葉
紋。〉　　總高約：23.8cm.　座底徑約：9.7cm.

Q-25
Middle of Ming Dynasty
About 15th Century

Blue Glaze of 4 Seasons Flower pattern octagonal 8 Bowls.
Height: 11.7cm.　Mouth Dia. in average: 25.5cm.　Foot rim Dia. in average: 13cm.
明中期　青花四季花卉八方碗
總高約：11.7cm.　平均口徑約：25.5cm.　平均圈足約：13cm.

O-1
Middle Ming Dynasty
About 15th Century

Blue Glaze of Unicorn / Banana Leaves / Stone pattern Jar. (with 4 direction medallion of Wave / Sea Beast design.)
Height over all : 32cm.　Mouth Dia. : 22.4cm.　Foot rim Dia. : 17cm.
明中期　青花麒麟蕉葉山石罐　〈肩繪浪濤海獸四面開光圖〉
總高約32cm.　口徑約22.4cm.　底徑約17cm.

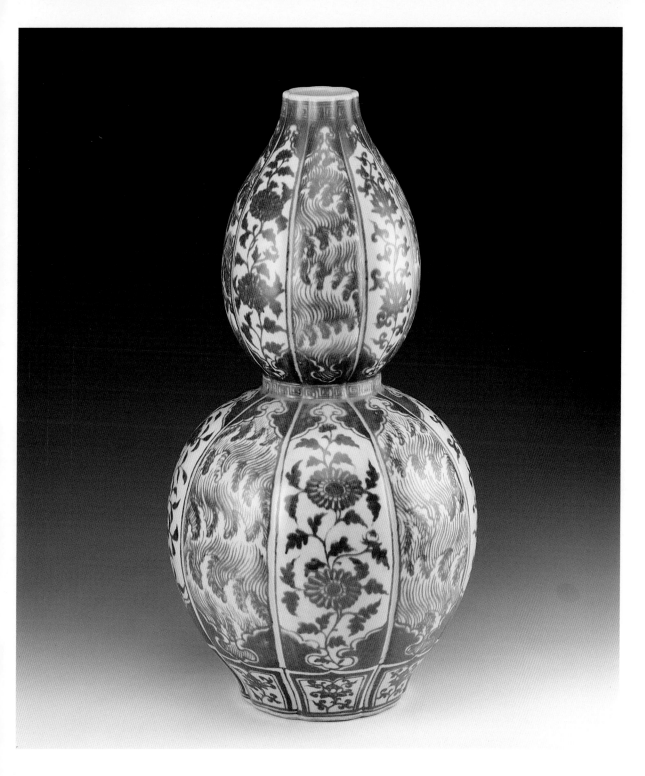

E-2
Ming Dynasty
About 14th Century

Underglazed Red of 8 Melon Ridge Double Gourd shaped Vase. With 8 layers of 16 surface patterns.
Height: 55.5cm. Mouth Dia.: 7cm. Foot rim Dia.: 15cm.
明中期　釉裡紅八瓣瓜楞型葫蘆瓶　〈瓶身總體分八層十六面繪飾〉
總高約55.5cm.　口徑約7cm.　圈足約15cm.

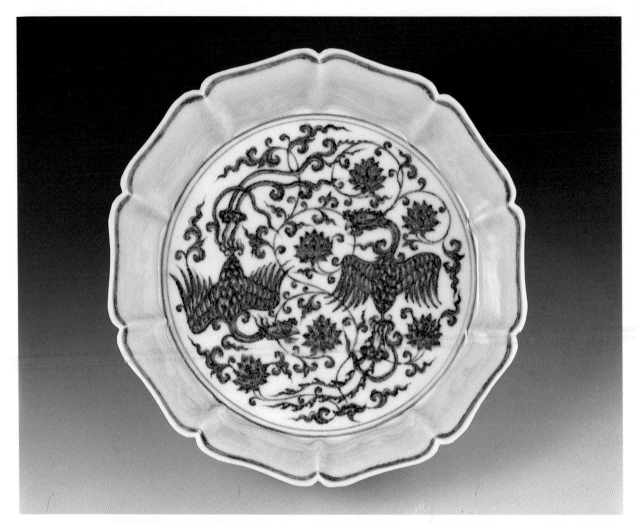

E-1
Middle of Ming Dynasty
About 15ᵗʰ Century

Blue Glaze of Phoenix design and in Caltrop shaped Edge Washer. With 10 Patels of Posy Phoenix and innerbottom of Double Phoenix / Interlocking branches Lily, also Phoenix & Interlocking branches Lily on outside.
Height: 5.4cm. Mouth Dia.: 19.2cm. Foot rim Dia.: 16.5cm.
明中期　青花鳳紋菱口洗　〈洗口分十瓣，每瓣皆繪飾團鳳紋，洗內底繪雙鳳纏枝蕃蓮紋，洗外底繪鳳紋纏枝〉
總高約5.4cm.　口徑約19.2cm.　底徑約16.5cm.

D-4
Middle Ming Dynasty
About 15ᵗʰ Century

Blue Glaze of Interlocking Flower with Hook shaped Ears Vase. With 7 layers of patterns：Banana Leaves at inner mouth, Rolled Grass on flared mouth and Interlocking branches and Flowers down to foot.
Height over all： 34cm. Mouth Dia.： 24.4cm. Foot rim Dia.： 17cm.
明中期　青花纏枝花卉出戟尊　〈全尊繪飾七層，尊口內繪蕉葉紋，尊外沿第一層繪捲草紋，第二至六層繪纏枝花卉紋〉
總高約34cm.　尊口徑約24.4cm.　底徑約17cm.

Q-29
Middle ～Later Ming Dynasty
About 16th Century

Blue Glaze of Cloud / Dragon / Phoenix pattern decorated with Double Elephant Head ears Vase.　With 7 layers of patterns：Triangular bow string, Banana Leaves, Cloud / Phoenix, Spiral Chrysanthemum, Subjective Cloud / Dragon, Brake and Interlocking Flower.　Height：36.9cm.　Mouth Dia.：10.6cm.　Foot rim Dia.：10.4cm.

明中後期　青花朵雲龍鳳紋雙耳象頭瓶　〈全器分七層繪飾，第一層繪三角弦紋，第二層繪蕉葉紋，第三層繪朵雲鳳鳥紋，第四層繪折枝菊花紋，第五層為瓶身主體繪朵雲龍紋，第六層繪鳳尾草紋，第七層繪纏枝花卉紋。〉

總高約：36.9cm.　口徑約：10.6cm.　圈足約：10.4cm.

Q-33
Middle or Later Ming Dynasty
About 16th Century

Blue Glaze of Banana Leaves / Figure Story pattern Double Eared Vase.
Height : 22.4cm.　Mouth Dia. : 6cm.　Foot rim Dia. : 6.7cm.
明中後期　青花蕉葉人物故事雙耳瓶
總高約：22.4cm.　口徑約：6cm.　底徑約：6.7cm.

N-1
Later Ming Dynasty
About 15th Century

Blue Glaze Double Eared in open work Double Phoenix pattern Vase. With 8 layers of pattern: Triangle oblique design, Banana Leaves, Spiral, Ru Yi then subjective open work Double Phoenix, coins and upset Ru Yi.
Height over all: 37.3cm. Mouth Dia.: 10.3cm. Foot rim Dia.: 10.7cm.
明中後期　青花雙耳穿花鳳凰瓶　〔瓶身總體分八層繪飾，第一層為三角形斜紋連續圖案，第二層為蕉葉紋，第三層為蓮紋，第四層為迴紋，第五層為如意紋，第六層為主圖穿花雙鳳圖，第七層為錢形紋，第八層為倒如意紋飾。〕
總高約37.3cm.　瓶口約10.3cm.　圈足約10.7cm.

78

Q-36
Ming Dynasty
About 15th Century

Blue Glaze of Sea Wave / Sanskrit character in octagonal Hook decorated Jar with cover.
Height with cover: 19.4cm.　Mouth Dia.: 12.5cm.　Base Dia.: 14cm.
明　青花海浪梵文八片形出戟罐
帶蓋總高約：19.4cm.　罐口徑約：12.5cm.　底徑約：14cm.

Q-12
Ming Dynasty, Era of Wan Li
About 1600 A.D.

Blue Glaze of Figure Story pattern Plate in pair. Marked with " Wan Li Nien Tse" 4 characters but is a civilian kiln production.
Height in average : 2.5cm. Mouth Dia. : about 12cm. Foot rim about : 8cm.
明萬曆民窯　青花人物故事盤一對　落萬曆年製四字款
平均高度約：2.5cm.　口徑約：12cm.　圈足約：8cm.

Q-7
Ming Dynasty, Era of Wan Li
About 1600 A.D.

Blue Glaze of Dragon pattern Square Food Box. Marked with " Ta Ming Wan Li Nien Tsc".
Height in average：13cm. Inner Dimension of Cover：25.5 × 25.2cm.
明萬曆　青花龍紋四方食盒　〔落大明萬曆年製款〕
平均總高約：13cm.　盒蓋內徑約：25.5cm. × 25.2cm.

H-5
Later Ming Dynasty
About 15th Century

Blue Glaze of Stone / Figure pattern Mei Ping.
Height: 20.2cm. Mouth Dia.: 4.4cm. Foot rim Dia.: 5cm.
明晚期　青花山石人物梅瓶　總高約20.2cm.　口徑約4.4cm.　圈足約5cm.

A-1
Latest Ming Dynasty
About 16th Century

Blue Glaze of Flower / 8 Precious items pattern Military Ewer.
Height over all : 15.5cm. Foot rim Dia. : 7.8cm.
明末　青花花卉八寶紋軍持瓶　總高約15.5cm.　圈足約7.8cm.

J-2
Ming Trade Porcelain

Blue Glaze of Dragon / Phoenix in flame pattern Jar.
Height: 16cm.　Mouth Dia.: 7cm.　Foot rim Dia.: 10cm.
明末　外貿瓷　青花龍鳳火焰紋罐
總高約16cm.　口徑約7cm.　圈足約10cm.

J-1
Ming Trade Porcelain

Blue Glaze of Flower / Character of Longevity Jar with Cover.
Height: 24cm.   Mouth Dia.: 9.8cm.   Foot rim Dia.: 14.5cm.
明末　外貿瓷　青花花卉壽字紋帶蓋罐
總高約24cm.　罐口徑約9.8cm.　圈足約14.5cm.

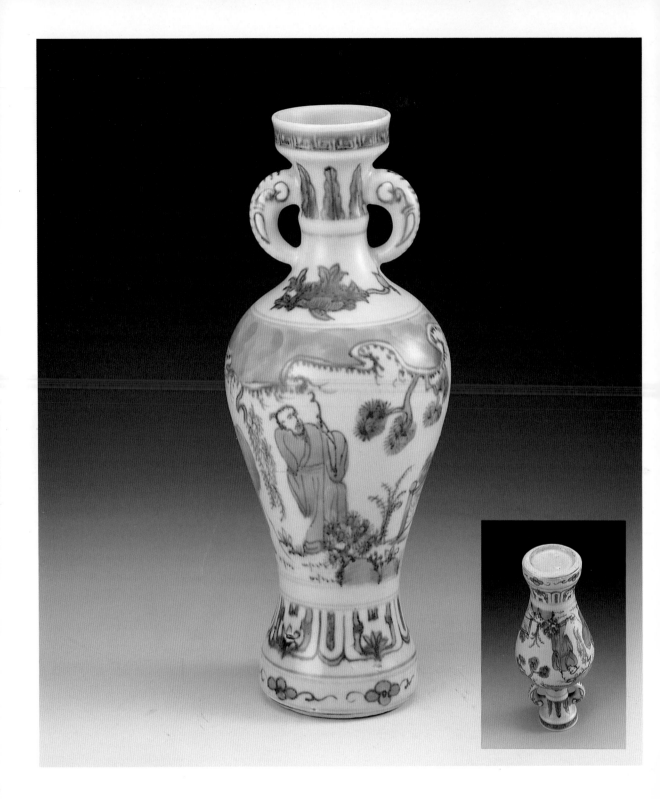

Q-10
Later Ming Dynasty
About 16th Century

Blue Glaze of Figure Story and Double Eared Elephant Head Designed Vase.
Height: 23.5cm.　Mouth Dia.: 4.9cm.　Inner Foot rim: 5.2cm.
明後期　青花人物故事雙耳象首瓶總高約：23.5cm.　口徑約：4.9cm.　圈足內徑約：5.2cm.

Q-21
Later Ming Dynasty
About 16th Century

Blue Glaze of Lion Knob Hexagonal Food Box with Cover.　Height： 21cm.
明後期　青花獅紐帶蓋六方食盒　帶蓋總高約：21cm.

Q-6
Later Ming Dynasty
About 16th Century

Blue Glaze of Figure pattern in design of 6 petal Brushers Holder.
Height over all: 14cm. Mouth Dia.: 19.5cm. Foot rim Dia.: 18.8cm.
明後期　青花人物六瓣型筆筒
總高約：14cm.　口徑約：19.5cm.　圈足約：18.8cm.

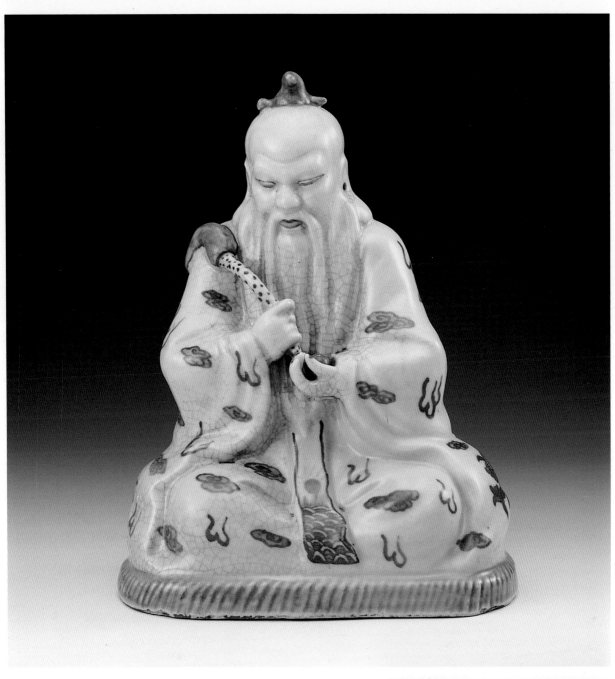

Q-45
Ming Dynasty
About 15th Century

Blue Glaze of Statue of Tai Shaun Lau Chuan.
Height over all: 26cm. Horizontal width on base: 20.1cm.
明　青花太上老君瓷塑像　總高約26cm　底橫長約20.1cm.

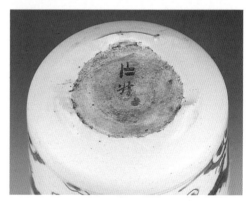

Q-40
17〜18th Century

Blue Glaze of Double Dragon striving Pearl pattern Incense Burner.　With 2 characters mark at bottom in black ink.
Height over all：10.2cm.　Mouth Dia.：12.6cm.
17〜18世紀　青花雙龍戲珠香爐　〈器底有墨書二字。〉
總高約：10.2cm.　口徑約：12.6cm.

Q-38
Ming to Ching Dynasties
About 16th Century

Blue Glaze of Figure / Landscape pattern with Floral flared edge Bowls in set of 4 pieces. Crane design at center of bowl.
Height in average : 6.6cm.   Mouth Dia. in average : 16.6cm.   Foot rim Dia. in average : 6.6cm.
明末〜清初　青花人物山水紋花口邊敞口碗外貿瓷四只一組　〈碗心繪鶴鳥紋。〉
平均高約：6.6cm.　平均口徑約：16.6cm.　平均圈足約：6.6cm.

Q-27
Ming ～Ching Dynasties
About 17th Century

Blue Glaze of Trade Porcelain Plate.
Height: 6.4cm. Mouth Dia.: 35.1cm. Foot rim Dia.: 18.8cm.
明～清初　青花外貿瓷盤
總高約：6.4cm.　盤口徑約：35.1ｍ.　圈足約：18.8cm.

Q-44

18th Century

Blue Glaze of Fungus pattern and veiled Eight Immortals design of Bodhidharma holding bowl. Height: 42.5cm.

18世紀　青花靈芝暗八仙紋持鉢達摩　總高約：42.5cm.

Q-9
Early Ching Dynasty
About 17ᵗʰ Century

Blue Glaze of " Figure " pattern Jar with cover.
Height over all: 11.5cm.　Mouth Dia.: 7.4cm.　Foot rim Dia.: 11.8cm.
清早期　青花人物帶蓋罐
連蓋總高：11.5cm.　口徑約：7.4cm.　圈足約：11.8cm.

Q-4
Early Ching Dynasty
About later 15th Century

Blue Glaze and Underglazed Red of Sea Wave Dragon / Flying Beast pattern Hat Covered Jar. With 6 layers including cover: Wave / Flying Beast on cover, Triangle pattern bow string pattern on cover edge, also triangle bow string pattern on Jar mouth edge, Lotus / Ruyi / Cloud Head and Subjective Sea Wave Dragon / Flying Beast and upset Lotus / Cloud pattern.
Height over all: 51cm. Mouth Dia.: 14.7cm. Foot rim Dia.: 19.5cm.
清早期　青花釉裡紅海水龍紋飛天獸將軍罐　〈罐身帶蓋，總體分六層繪飾，第一層罐蓋繪海水飛天獸，第二層罐蓋邊沿繪三角形弦紋，第三層罐口邊沿繪三角形弦紋，第四層繪蓮花如意雲頭紋，第五層主體繪海水龍紋飛天獸，第六層繪倒蓮雲紋。〉
帶蓋總高約：51cm.　罐口徑約：14.7cm.　圈足約：19.5cm.

Q-35
Early Ching Dynasty
About 16th Century

Blue Glaze of Chinese Scholors 4 games： Lute, Cheese, Writing and Painting pattern Brusher Holder.
Height： 15.3cm.　Mouth Dia.： 18.7cm.　Base Dia.： 18.3cm.
清早期　青花琴、棋、書、畫，雅士圖筆筒
總高約：15.3cm.　口徑約：18.7cm.　底徑約：18.3cm.

Q-19
Early Ching Dynasty
About 16th Century

Blue Glaze of 3 Winter Friends pattern Jar with cover.
Marked with blue double circle.
Height with cover: 24cm. Mouth Dia.: 9.7cm. Foot rim Dia.: 13.6cm.
清早期　青花歲寒三友帶蓋罐　落青花雙圈款
帶蓋總高約：24cm.　口徑約：9.7m.　圈足約：13.6cm.

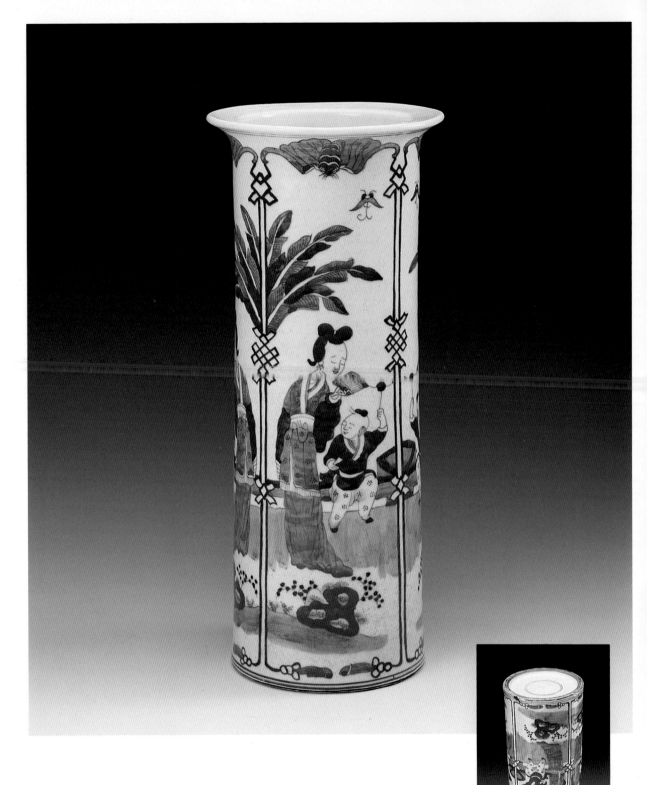

Q-51
Early Ching Dynasty
About 17th Century

Blue Glaze of Figure Story Folded Rim Scroll / paper Holder.
Height： 34.5cm. Mouth Dia.： 15.2cm. Foot rim Dia.： 12.4cm.
清早期　青花人物故事折沿筒瓶
總高約：34.5cm. 口徑約：15.2cm. 圈足約：12.4cm.

Q-8
Early Ching Dynasty
About 17ᵗʰ Century

Blue Glaze of " Figure " pattern Brushers Holder. Marked with blue in
double circle.
Height over all : 13.5cm. Mouth Dia. : 10.5cm. Foot rim Dia. : 8.8cm.
清早期　青花人物筆筒　落青花雙圈款
總高約：13.5cm.　口徑約：10.5cm.　圈足約：8.8cm.

Q-50
Ching Dynasty, Era of Yung Cheng
About 1720 A.D.

Blue Glaze of Sea Wave / Interlocking Flowers pattern Folded Rim Basin. Marked with : "Ta Ching Yung Cheng Nien Tse" 6 orthodox characters in double circle.
Height: 10cm. Mouth Dia.: 25.5cm. Base Dia.: 18.5cm.
清雍正　青花浪濤纏枝花卉紋折沿盤　落大清雍正年製六字楷書雙圈款
總高約：10cm.　口徑約：25.5cm.　底徑約：18.5cm.

Q-15
Ching Dynasty, Era of Chian Lung
About 1750 A.D.

Blue Glaze with Double Medallion of Spring Plow of double eared Dear
Head decorated Vase. Marked with " Ta Ching Chian Lung Nien Tse"
6 seal script blue characters.
Height over all：22.7cm. Mouth Dia.：11.6cm. Foot rim Dia.：13cm.
清乾隆　青花雙面開光春耕圖雙耳鹿頭尊　落大清乾隆年製六字篆書青花款
總高約：22.7cm. 口徑約：11.6cm. 底徑約：13cm.

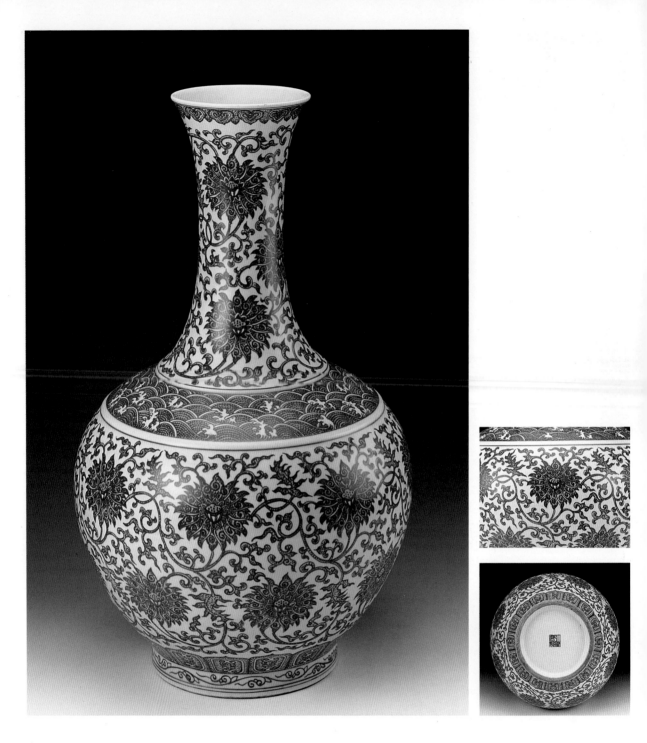

F-2
Ching Dynasty
Era of Chian Lung (1750)

Blue Glaze of Interlocking branches Lily pattern Decorative Vase. With 6 layers of pattern: Ru Yi on outside flared mouth edge. Interlocking branches on neck, Sea Wave on shoulder, Interlocking branches Lily on belly, Lotus patel at lower and Rolled Grass near foot.
Height over all: 53cm. Mouth Dia.: 13.2cm. Foot rim Dia.: 17.7cm.
清乾隆　青花纏枝蕃蓮紋賞瓶　〈罐身總體分六層繪飾，第一層瓶口外沿繪如意紋，第二層瓶頸繪纏枝蕃蓮紋，第三層瓶肩繪海浪紋，第四層瓶腹繪纏枝蕃蓮紋，第五層瓶下部繪蓮瓣紋，第六層瓶足部繪捲草紋〉
總高約53cm. 口徑約13.2cm. 圈足約17.7cm.

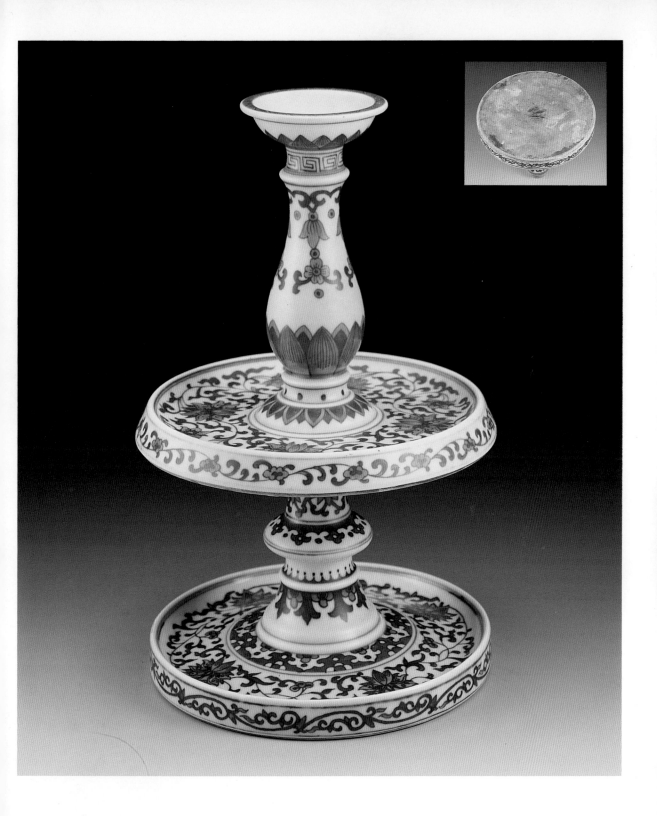

Q-22
Middle of Ching Dynasty
About 18ᵗʰ Century

Blue Glaze of Interlocking Lily pattern with 2 layers mortised type Candle Stay.
Height: 26cm.   Mouth Dia.of Hole: 6.8cm.
清中期　青花纏枝蕃蓮紋二層榫式燭臺　總高約：26cm.　燭臺口徑約：6.8cm.

Q-26
Ching Dynasty
About 19th Century

Blue Glaze of Poem on Book Leaf pattern Brusher Holder. Civilian Kiln prod
Height：19cm. Mouth Dia.：18.2cm. Foot rim Dia.：18.2cm.
清道光民窯　青花山水詩句書頁式筆筒
總高約：19cm. 口徑約：18.2m. 圈足約：18.2cm.

J-3
Ching Dynasty
Era of Kwang Hsu (1890)

Blue Glaze of Flower / Stone / Bird pattern Gall shaped Bottle. Marked with "Ta Ching Kwang Hsu Nien Tse" 6
blue orthodox characters.x
Height: 20.5cm. Mouth Dia.: 2.8cm. Foot rim Dia.: 6cm.
清　青花花卉山石鳥禽紋膽瓶　〈落大清光緒年製六字楷書青花款〉
總高約20.5cm.　瓶口徑約2.8cm.　圈足約6cm.

L-1
19th Century

Japanese Ancient Atlas pattern of relief carved with Double Crane and Sea WaveLarge Plate.   Marked with " Tien Pao
Nien Tse" 4 orthodox characters in blue.
Mouth Dia.: 39.9cm.   Height: 7.8cm.   Foot rim Dia.: 25cm.
19世紀　中國貿易瓷日本古地圖青花浮雕古地名雙鶴海浪紋飾盤　〈落日本年號，青花款，天保年製四字楷書款〉
口徑約39.9cm.　總高約7.8cm.　圈足約25cm.

Q-57 (特1)
Ming ～Ching Dynasties
About 17ᵗʰ Century

Blue Glaze of Wavy Finish Furnace Transmutation Jar.　(Originally of Hundred Dears Design - can see dear's horn, but glaze of Blue was waved and spread by forming a special pattern glaze of Blue was waved and spread by forming a special pattern on Jar.)　Height over all : 33.5cm.　Mouth Dia. : 13.4cm.　Foot rim Dia. : 14.8cm.

明～清　青花暈染（窯變）罐　〈本器物原始應繪百鹿圖案，《部份地方尚可見鹿角圖案》在窯燒時青花藍料暈散而形成另一風格之青花特色之罐〉。

總高約：33.5cm.　口徑約：13.4cm.　圈足約：14.8cm.

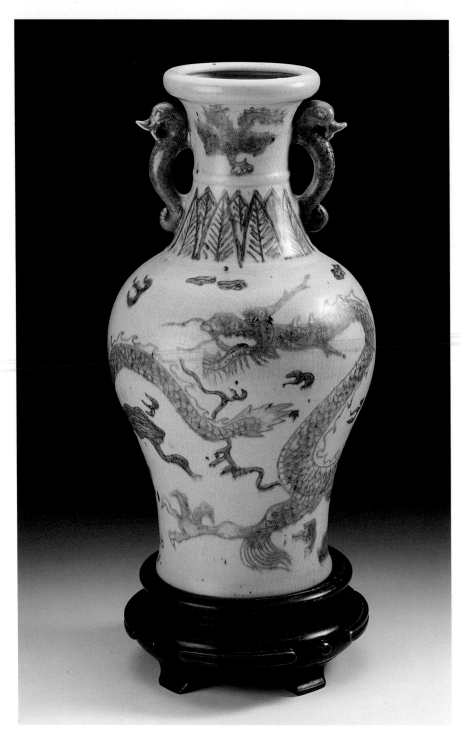

Q-58 (特2)
Yuan ～Ming Dynasties
About 13th Century

Underglazed Red / Blue Glaze of Cloud / Dragon / Phoenix / Banana Leaf pattern Double Eared Vase.
Height: 33.6cm. Mouth Dia.: 10.5cm. Foot rim Dia.: 12cm.
元～明 青花釉裡紅朵雲龍鳳蕉葉紋雙耳瓶
高約：33.6cm. 口徑約：10.5cm. 圈足約：12cm.

Q-59　(特3)
Yuan ～ Ming Dyansties
About 13th Century

Underglazed Red of Interlocking Branches Floral pattern Plate.　With 3 layers of pattern : Moslem Characters, Squares Design and subjective Interlocking Branches / Floral.　On outer edge decorated with 19
petals of Lotus / Cloud design.
Mouth Dia. : 30.5cm.　Height : 4.6cm.　Foot rim Dia. : 18.9cm.
元～明　釉裡紅纏枝花卉紋盤　〈盤內沿分三層繪飾，第一層繪回紋，第二層繪方勝紋，第三層繪主體纏枝花卉紋；
盤外沿繪11格蓮瓣朵雲紋〉。
盤口徑約：30.5cm.　高約：4.6cm.　圈足約：18.9cm.

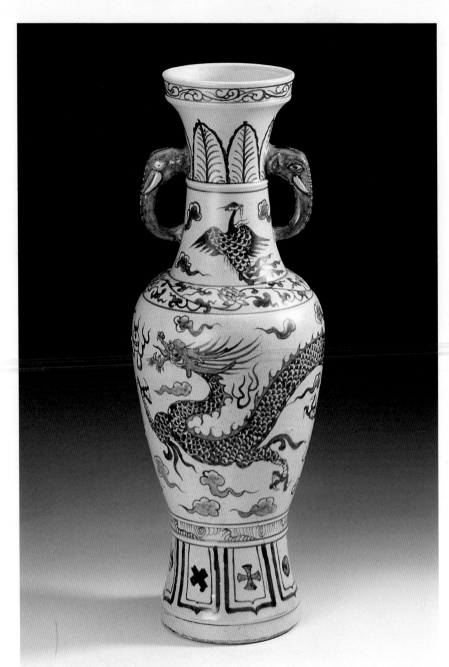

Q-60　(特4)
Yuan Dynasty
About 13th Century

Blue Glaze of Dragon / Phoenix and cloud pattern decorated with double ears of Elephant Head design
Vase.　With 7 layers of pattern : Rolled Grass, Banana Leaves　(61 characters in blue on other side) ,
Cloud / Phoenix tail and Lotus petal with precious items pattern.
Height over all : 62cm.　Mouth Dia. : 14.8cm.　Foot rim Dia. : 16cm.
元　青花龍鳳朵雲紋雙耳象首瓶　〈瓶身總體分七層繪飾，第一層繪捲草紋，第二層繪蕉葉紋《另面有青花書寫61
字。》，第三層繪朵雲鳳紋，第四層繪纏枝蓮紋，第五層繪朵雲龍紋，第六層繪鳳尾紋，第七層繪蓮瓣吉祥紋。〉
總高約：62cm.　口徑約：14.8cm.　圈足約：16cm.

110

國家圖書館出版品預行編目資料

中國歷代青花瓷精選集 ╱ 王興祖總編輯.
初版. ‐ 臺北市 ：東業國際，民85
120面；18.7 x 27公分
ISBN 957-99252-0-8　（精裝）

1. 陶瓷 ‐ 古物 ‐ 中國 ‐ 圖錄

796.6   85000243

Selections of Chinese Historical Blue Glazed Porcelain.
-Edited by H.T. Wang-
      First Edition　(De Luxe)
      Sunrise International, 1996
      ISBN　957-99252-0-8

I　Ceramics　Relics　Chinese　Pictorial Illustration.

      796.6   85000243

中國歷代青花瓷精選集 (一)

總 編 輯： 王興祖
主　　編： 蔡養吾
執行編輯： 王碧瑛
企劃總監： 胡正群
編　　輯： 呂紫紅 鍾啟文
美術編輯： 蒲公英廣告事業有限公司
攝　　影： 曹以松
出 版 者： 東業國際圖書出版股份有限公司
發 行 人： 詹仲琦
公　　司： 臺北市忠孝東路2段88號B1
電　　話： (02) 396-5756
傳　　真： (02) 351-6279
郵政信箱： 台北郵政84-179號信箱 王興祖先生收
郵政劃撥： 一八七七五四六三東業國際圖書出版股份有限公司
國內總經銷： 三友圖書有限公司
　　　　　　 台北縣中和市中山路2段327巷11弄17號5樓
　　　　　　 TEL：(02) 240-5600　FAX：(02) 240-9284
印　　刷： 名頂企業股份有限公司
製　　版： 永益彩色製版印刷有限公司
定　　價： 新臺幣壹千貳百元整
中華民國八十五年十二月一日初版
行政院新聞局核准登記證局版北市業字第二零一號
版權所有‧翻印必究

Selections of Chinese Historical Blue Glazed Porcelain　(I)

Chief Publisher：Hsing Tsu Wang
Chief Editor：Orlando Tsai
Executive Editor：Pi-Ying Wang
Executive of Projecting　：Jeng Chyun Hwu
Editor：T.H. Leu, Chiwen Chung
Art Editior：Dandelion Advertising Corp.
Photographer：Tsao I Sung
Publisher：Sunrise International Publication Corp.
Publisher：Chan Chung Chi
Address：B1, 88 Chung Hsiao E. Rd. Sec.2, Taipei
Telephone：886-2-396-5756
Fax：886-2-351-6279
P.O.Box：84-179 Taipei, Taiwan, R.O.C.
　　　　To：Mr.Hsing Tsu Wang
Price：NT$1,200 Per Copy
First Edition：Dec. 1. 1996
License：PEI - YIH 201